DREAM
SYMBOLS

DREAM SYMBOLS

Understanding the Secret Language of the Dreamlife

JUDITH MILLIDGE

BARNES
&NOBLE
BOOKS
NEW YORK

p2, clockwise from top left: Railway tracks through a tunnel suggest a direct route to the unconscious; a Raggedy Ann doll, associated with childhood security; gateways, a universal emblem of passage and transition; the nightmarish Medusa, by Caravaggio.

Right: *Dream Improvisation (1913), by Wassily Kandinsky.*

For Chloe and Lottie— Sweet Dreams!

This edition published by Barnes and Noble, Inc., by arrangement with Saraband Inc.

Copyright © 1998 Saraband Inc.

Design © Ziga Design
Editor: Robin Langley Sommer
Art director: Charles J. Ziga
Graphic designer: Wendy Ciaccia
Photo editors: Sara Hunt, Nicola Gillies

Library of Congress Cataloging in Publication data available

ISBN: 0-7607-0888-6

Printed in China

10 9 8 7 6 5 4 3 2 1

Contents

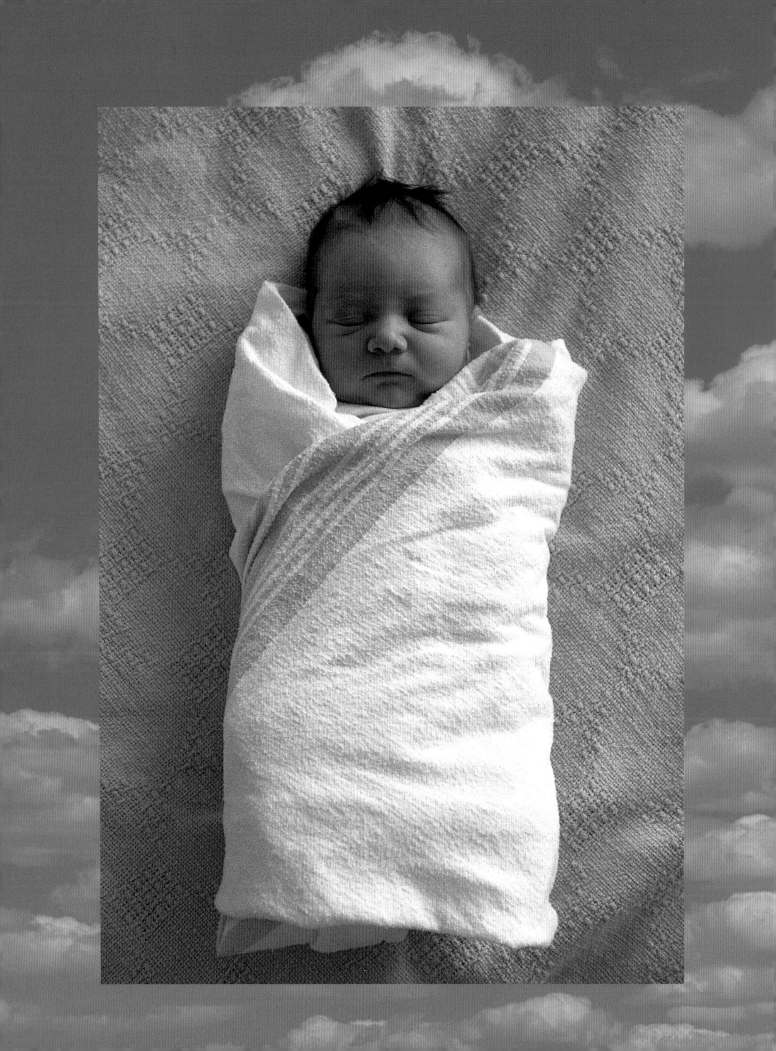

Introduction

Everyone dreams, but few of us really know what our dreams mean, or indeed whether they are in any way important. While individual opinions on the significance of dream images vary widely, no one disputes that such images are quite incredible. The subconscious imagination can produce impressions and ideas that often amaze (and sometimes horrify) the conscious mind. Our sleeping minds roam across continents both real and fantastic, speak to people long dead or simply imaginary, and conjure up stories that professional novelists would envy. In the cold light of day, however, dreams often appear both baffling and nonsensical.

THE STUFF THAT DREAMS ARE MADE OF

It does not seem logical to credit the ramblings of the sleeping mind with any significance for the conscious mind, and today, scientists and psychologists are sharply divided in their attitudes to the importance of dreams. One thing is clear: laboratory tests have proved that when an individual who has been deprived of sleep is allowed to sleep normally, he or she displays signs of an increased amount of REM (Rapid Eye Movement), the physical sign that a person is dreaming. It seems that not only will the body sleep longer to compensate for fatigue, the mind will also dream more—and perhaps more intensely. Sleep is vital to our well-being, and this evidence suggests that dreams are too. Our brains go on "thinking" while we sleep, using non-verbal means to process thoughts and images.

Dreams can be seen as conversations we have with ourselves, as it were, in a symbolic language that sends messages from the unconscious to the conscious mind. The best potential interpreter of a dream is probably the dreamer him- or herself, providing he or she has learned to recognize elements in this language, since only the dreamer will understand the personal implications of every symbol thrown up by the unconscious mind. Symbols in dreams do not have one universal interpretation. Their meaning depends on the context in which they occur, and to some extent on the particular meaning they have for the individual. Though many symbols have a recognized meaning, individuals

Opposite: *Life's journey begins with deep and frequent sleep, as the infant connects with the world around it, then subsides into rest—and dreaming.*

Below: *A scientist studies the sleep patterns of a volunteer at a research facility in Bethesda, Maryland.*

Right: A Chinese dream landscape of pavilions, natural features and a distant horizon.

Below: A businessman feels that he is walking a tightrope in his waking life, balancing his skills against the whims of the marketplace.

superimpose their own subjective attitudes, emotions and experience, and develop a kind of personal symbolic shorthand. In addition, different cultures apply different meanings to objects.

It is also important to recognize the differences between literal dreams and symbolic ones. Many dreams repeat actions or events of our waking life and are not laden with great symbolic meaning. A dream about decorating the house just a few hours after folding up the wall-papering table is probably not a message from the subconscious about caring for the soul— which might be indicated in another context. More likely, the mind is running

through the events of the day. Literal dreams like this also allow us to reassess incidents or situations that may have seemed puzzling during waking hours. Sigmund Freud (1856–1939) put it simply when he wrote: "A thing in a dream means what it recalls to the mind."

People of all cultures are intrigued by the purpose of dreams. In the ancient world, they were recorded almost as soon as literacy became prevalent. They have been studied avidly for thousands of years, at least since the Babylonian epic of Gilgamesh, which was inscribed on stone tablets some 6,000 years before the birth of Christ.

All ancient civilizations and cultures had theories about dreams and their interpretation. The Egyptians and Babylonians believed that dreams were caused by gods or demons; the ancient Chinese regarded them as experiences of the soul, which wandered during sleep. The ancient Greeks were the first to believe that dreams are the result of normal mental activity during sleep, a theory accepted widely, but not universally, today.

Many African societies believe that dreams are sent by their ancestors to advise and warn them. The Zulus pool their dreams and refer to their tribal dream interpreters as "head men." Most Native American tribes actively advocate dreaming. Children are encouraged to remember and explore their dreams from an early age, and "dream catching" became part of the initiation ceremonies of certain tribes. "Dream festivals" were integral to Huron and Iroquois culture, wherein dreams were shared and the pattern that emerged was used to construct tribal policy. Dreams are believed to convey messages from ancestors by some tribes, while for others, they can fulfill a healing function.

Australian Aborigines hold to their traditional belief in the "dreamtime"—the period in which the visible landscape was created and all life had its source. They believe that their spiritual ancestors, who were born of the earth, traveled across Australia depositing the spirits of unborn children. After passing on to humans the knowledge necessary for survival, these ethereal creatures disappeared back into the earth. The waterholes they created became sacred sites, and stories of their journeys are passed down the generations in Aboriginal oral tradition. The dreamtime, or dreaming, can be re-entered through rituals in which the participants identify with their early ancestors and relive "the strong time of creation."

Anthropologists have distinguished four basic types of dream among ancient cultures: "big" dreams having cultural significance; prophetic dreams warning of future events; medical dreams that promote healing; and "little" dreams of significance only to the dreamer. Primitive peoples valued "big" dreams above all, believing that they gave access to supernatural wisdom and guidance. These dreams were invaluable to shamans and medicine men, providing them with the power to heal, divine the future and recover souls. Ironically, the dreams most people dwell on today are the "little" ones of personal interest, which were regarded as trivial by our ancestors.

The discovery that archetypal dreams occurred all over the world over a timespan of thousands of years provided the basis for the theory of the collective unconscious, propounded by Carl Jung (1875–1961). After much research, he came to believe that humankind shared a deep well of images and stories that acted as common building blocks and symbols in all our dreams.

Left: A Native American "dream catcher," believed to ensnare evil spirits that might harm the sleeper, and, among some tribes, to transmit messages from benign powers who provide guidance through dreams.

Left: Ayers Rock, Northern Territory, called Uluru (great pebble), is a sacred site for Australia's nomadic Aboriginal peoples. As they travel the arid wilderness from one waterhole to another, they pass on their oral traditions of the "dreamtime," when their world was created, and re-enter that time through rituals and rock paintings enshrined by this sandstone monolith.

EARLY CIVILIZATIONS

The earliest records of dreams are from the Babylonian dream books discovered in King Ashurbanipal's library, dating from the sixth century BC. *The Epic of Gilgamesh,* inscribed on clay tablets, is full of accounts of dreams. The legend features Gilgamesh, King Uruk, a monarch troubled by stunningly vivid nightmares. The Babylonians were obsessed by dreams, believing that they were sent by demons and spirits; in order to protect themselves from such malign influences they built temples to Mamu, goddess of dreams. They regarded their night visions primarily as warnings: to dream of flying, for example, was a warning of impending disaster.

The Egyptians also treated dreams as warnings, but believed they came directly from the gods rather than via spirit intermediaries or minor deities in the pantheon. In return for sacrifices and penance, the gods would answer dreamers' questions; these experiences were generally regarded as forces for good. Dreams were often interpreted in terms of meaningful opposites, so hideous nightmares could indicate that good times were ahead, while happy dreams could portend something dreadful. Dream symbols were understood either through rhyming word sounds, or through association, a forerunner of the modern "free association" method of interpretation. Egyptian civilization was the first known to have practiced dream incubation to promote healing, in temples dedicated to the god Imhotep. Serapis, the god of dreams, had many temples, the most famous at Memphis, dating from about 3000 BC; the earliest account of dream interpretation dates from 1350 BC.

The ancient Greeks shared the Egyptian tradition of healing via dream incubation with the help of Aesklepius, the god of healing. At the height of his cult, 300 of his temples were scattered throughout Greece. Surrounded by woods and sacred streams, and located close to the sea, they were places of great beauty. There patients underwent ritual purification before entering the *abaton*, the sacred place of the gods, which was full of harmless snakes. Under the influence of a sleeping draught, and the god Hypnos, the patient slept and was visited in his dreams by Aesklepius. The god's appearance was enough to promote healing, and no interpretation of the dream was necessary. It was believed that Aesklepius summoned sacred snakes to lick the wounds of the afflicted dreamer and so cure them, and his symbol, the caduceus—two snakes entwined around a staff—is still used to represent healing.

The earliest recorded Greek observer of dreams was the philosopher Heraclitus (450–375 BC), who wrote "For the waking there is one common world only; but when asleep, each man turns to his own private world." He would have supported the theory that dream symbolism is based very heavily on one's personal experiences. Hippocrates (460–377 BC) believed that dreams could warn patients of impending illness or death via symbolic representation: to dream of floods, for example, suggested the presence of too much blood and implied that the dreamer needed bleeding. He also accepted the importance of astrological and divine influences, a view not shared by Aristotle (384–322 BC), who argued that this was impossible because animals dreamed too. Aristotle's views come closer to modern attitudes than those of any writer before him, and most since, yet despite his incredible influence on Western civilization and thought, his views on dreams were neglected for the better part of 2,000 years. His observation that the hallucinations of mental patients and the dreams of ordinary people had much in common, and might therefore have a shared origin, anticipated Jung. Plato (427-347 BC) argued that in dreams we do things we would be ashamed to do in reality: "The virtuous man is content to *dream* what a wicked man really *does.*" This foreshadowed Freud's theory that all dreams represented some form of wish-fulfillment.

The first researcher to devote his life to a study of dreams was the Roman philosopher Artemidorus of Daldus (AD 138–180), who traveled all over Italy, Greece and the Near East to explore everything that was known about dreams at that time. He found King Ashurbanipal's ancient stone tablets in Nineveh, capital of the ancient Assyrian empire. He interviewed dream interpreters and considered every aspect of a dream before proffering an interpretation. Artemidorus was the first to ascribe importance to the interpretation of symbols in dreams, noting that dreams could rarely be taken at face value. His book *The Interpretation of Dreams* established the occurrence and reoccurrence of the same dream symbols and the existence of a few fundamental types of dream. It provides a link between ancient methods of dream interpretation and modern attitudes. Freud was the first to recognize the importance of Artemidorus's study, and, nearly two thousand years later, endowed his seminal work with the same title.

"I CANNOT GRASP ALL THAT I AM"

Despite the perennial interest in dreams, it is not too sweeping a generalization to say that no one produced any really influential work on the subject from the days of Artemidorus until the eighteenth century. Philosophers and writers made pronouncements on the origin and meaning of dreams, but there were no great studies to rival those of Artemidorus or even Aristotle.

The grip of the Roman Catholic Church on the conscious and subconscious mind of medieval Western Europe severely limited serious studies of dreams. Although the church fathers of the fourth century AD believed that dreams could be divinely inspired, Christian orthodoxy altered as time went by. St. Augustine (AD 354–430), that most human of saints, realized that part of his functioning mind was the unconscious and that his rational self had little grasp of what it contained, and probably even less control over the thoughts it threw up. "I cannot grasp all that I am," he wrote, fearing that God would punish him for his worldly dreams.

The Christian theologian Gregory of Nyassa (AD 331–395), in the treatise entitled *On the Making of Man*, stated that dreams occur in sleep because the rational intellect is at rest. He believed that dreams are influenced by the day's activities and the physical state of the dreamer at a given time. Because the intellect is resting, the dream mind, governed by the passions (what he called "man's brute nature"), runs riot, producing images normally restrained by the intellect. Gregory's theories are a startling forerunner of the Freudian theory that all dreams are essentially wish-fulfillment.

In the thirteenth century, believers were told that as the future was solely in the hands of God, dreams could not be prophetic, nor were they harbingers of divine messages. The scholar and theologian St. Thomas Aquinas (1225–74) distinguished between divine revelations and "unlawful and superstitious dreams." The extent of the Church's unease about the importance attached to dreams is seen in the repressive way it reacted to cases like Joan of Arc. People who claimed their dreams were divinely inspired were condemned as blasphemous. A fervent woman who combined missionary zeal with a popular message, Joan of Arc saw visions of saints from the age of thirteen, and heard voices telling her to serve the French dauphin and expel the English from France. She was burned at the stake in 1431 as a heretical witch, partly because Church authorities denied that her dreams or visions could be divinely inspired.

Popular interest in dream interpretation, however, was very strong and never really declined, although there was little formal work on the subject until the Renaissance. From the fifteenth century, with the advent of printing, dream dictionaries proliferated, based mainly on the work of

Below: Joan of Arc, a dreamer whose visions changed the course of French history. Her claim to divine guidance through dreams was condemned by Church authorities and played a part in her execution on grounds of heresy and witchcraft.

Far left: *St. Augustine of Hippo, the early Church Father whose writings had a decisive influence on Christian tradition for centuries. He believed that dreams could be divinely inspired, but Christian orthodoxy moved away from this theory.* **Left:** *By the sixteenth century, Protestant reformer Martin Luther was teaching his followers that dreams revealed their sinful nature.*

Artemidorus. First published in England in 1518, the classic went through twenty editions in the ensuing 200 years. Despite this popular interest, ascetic Protestants gave no credence to their dreams: Martin Luther, for example, was sure that his nighttime lusts were the work of the devil. The seventeenth-century philosopher Thomas Hobbes believed that dreams were governed by the physical body. "There can happen in sleep," he wrote, "… no dream, but what proceeds from the agitation of the inward parts of a man's body."

As literacy became more widespread, popular pamphlets and tracts appeared, some with humorous comments and drawings about dreams. More serious essayists realized that dreams were important, but as the seventeenth-century English Platonist John Norris (1632–1704) wrote, "there are infinitely more ideas impressed on our minds than we can possibly attend to or perceive."

The German Romantic Movement of the late eighteenth century developed various theories on dreaming. By the end of the century, dreams were recognized as products of the unconscious, which was itself an expression of nature, credited as the source of all creative and imaginative ideas. The German physicist G.C. Lichtenberg (1742–99) was the first scholar to link dreams with the unconscious; he studied his dreams simply because he found them to be full of wonderful ideas.

In England, Henry Maudsley established a reputation as a physician of "nervous disorders," and his 1867 work *Pathology of Mind* was, in most respects, a conventional treatise on neurophysiology. However, he broke away from accepted thought in marvelling at the power of the sleeping mind to arrange ideas into "the most vivid dramas." He also noticed that "dreams are sometimes found to go before a severe bodily illness which they seem to foretell," but despite his observations, none of his peers was interested in the possible therapeutic power of dreams.

Right: Sigmund Freud, the father of modern dream interpretation.
Below: Archetypes transcend both time and place, as seen in these images of mother and child, from Africa, at left, to contemporary Europe, in the Renoir painting at right.

FREUD AND JUNG

The more extreme aspects of Freudian dream theory are questioned today, but all serious researchers acknowledge the great debt owed to the Austrian originator of psychoanalysis.

Though he built on the ideas and theories extant at the time, he also made a great leap forward in his advocacy of wish-fulfillment as the basis for all dreams and in his examination of symbolism. His achievement was twofold: first, his identification of dreams as products of the subconscious, which overrides the censoring conscious during sleep by the use of symbols; second, he advocated the method of free association as a means of interpreting dreams and their symbols.

Freud trained in neurology and followed his colleague Josef Breuer (1842–1925) in using hypnosis to treat cases of hysteria. He began to explore his patients' dreams for clues to their problems, a subject that occupied him throughout the 1890s. In 1895 he decided that all dreams express the fulfillment of a hidden wish.

It is hard to underestimate the impact of Freud's central thesis when it was published in 1899 in *The Interpretation of Dreams*: "The interpretation of dreams is the royal road to a knowledge of the unconscious activities of the mind." Scientists scoffed at his work, and Freud spent much of his career reacting against the standard belief of the time that dreams (particularly those of the mentally unstable patients with whom he was involved) were worthless and trivial. Ultimately, his theory would have a profound effect on the psychological approach to dreaming throughout the twentieth century.

Although he professed that "I have no theory about dreams," Carl Jung's dreams played an important part in his own career, often providing the solution to problems at critical points in his work. Jung worked closely with Freud from 1907 until 1913, but their differences were clear as early as 1911, when Jung published his first important work, *Psychology of the Unconscious*, a study that deviated from Freudian orthodoxy in several respects. Jung believed that Freud's emphasis on wish-fulfillment was too constricting, and that there was much more to dreams, including "ineluctable

RELIGIOUS DREAMS

Although the Bible is filled with important dreams, Christianity as a faith put little or no trust in them until relatively recently. Ancient Jewish tradition was more receptive, and emphasized the importance of the individual dreamer's life circumstances, anticipating Jung. In Biblical times, Jewish scholars enjoyed an excellent reputation as dream interpreters and were often employed by the pharaohs of Egypt for this purpose. In the Old Testament, Joseph made it clear that Pharaoh's dream of seven fat and seven lean cattle represented seven fruitful years followed by seven years of famine.

Left: Carl Jung, who formulated the theory of archetypes and the collective unconscious in the early twentieth century. Below: Raphael's Ezekiel's Vision depicts the winged creatures described in the Old Testament Book of Ezekiel, which would be identified by Christian converts from Judaism as types of the Four Evangelists.

truths,…philosophical pronouncements, irrational experiences, even telepathic visions and heaven knows what besides."

Jung's wide knowledge of comparative religion and mythology convinced him that cultures separated by thousands of miles and hundreds of years shared common themes. This was the beginning of his celebrated theory of the collective unconscious. He called the primordial images common to dreams, legends and myths the world over "archetypes," and believed that they were transmitted in a way analogous to that by which physical characteristics pass from generation to generation. In his method of dream interpretation, Jung operated on three levels, approaching dreams from personal, archetypal and cultural angles so as to amplify the meaning of the symbols produced by each dreamer. This represented a considerable departure from Freud's rigid interpretations, in which he assigned fixed meanings to symbols and insisted that as life energy was primarily sexual, dreams must, in turn, relate to sex. This disagreement was the main cause of the break between Freud and Jung, although Jung continued to acknowledge the importance of Freud's work.

Right and below: Mystical images from Hinduism and Christianity. Right, the compassionate Buddha in the blissful state of Nirvana. Below, a vision of the twelfth-century German mystic Hildegard of Bingen, who classified her dreams as either prophetic or mundane.

Similarly, Daniel displayed exceptional skill and discretion in interpreting Nebuchadnezzar's megalomaniac dream. In the New Testament, an angel appeared to Joseph in a dream to tell him of Jesus' immaculate conception and Mary's innocence. In another dream, Joseph was warned of Herod's impending massacre of male children with the urgent message, "Get up, take the child and his mother, and flee to Egypt" (Matthew 2:13).

Muslims believe that the prophet Muhammad founded Islam after a dream in Mecca, Arabia, showed him that he had been chosen to join the great prophets. In AD 610, a majestic being later identified as the angel Gabriel led Muhammad on a silvery mare first to Jerusalem and then to heaven, where he met Christ, Adam and the four Evangelists. The revelations Muhammad received became the basis of a new faith, with its spiritual center at Medina. Muhammad told his followers that good visions were a sign of Allah's blessing, and bad ones came from the devil.

Siddhartha Gautama, the wealthy young Indian who became Buddha, received his inspiration for enlightenment in a dream. A passage on dream interpretation in the ancient Hindu text *Atharva Veda* states that in a series of dreams, only the last one is significant. Hindu tradition also notes the importance of individual dream images, relating them to a wider system of symbols that reflect the symbolic attributes of gods and demons.

INSPIRATIONAL DREAMS

Dreams have featured in legends, literature and art for centuries, irrespective of the importance ascribed to dreaming by the culture in which they were created. Shakespeare's plays, for example, are riddled with references to dreams and sleep. Lady Macbeth is seen sleep-walking and showing remorse in her dreams; Hamlet muses upon the links between sleep and death; and the characters in *A Midsummer Night's Dream* are a bizarre mixture of real people and enchanting fairies who create mischief in both dimensions of the play.

John Bunyan's *The Pilgrim's Progress* is written in the allegorical form of a dream. In the eighteenth century, such visionaries as William Blake rejected the rationalist theories of the Enlightenment and let their imaginations roam free (occasionally inspired by stimulants other than snuff). Many of Blake's poems were meshed inextricably with his dreams. He illustrated Dante's *Divine Comedy*, and his own *Songs of Innocence and Experience*, with an amazing set of nightmarish, almost surreal, pictures.

Samuel Taylor Coleridge conjured up the unforgettable images of *Kubla Khan* after a restless sleep:

> *In Xanadu did Kubla Khan*
> *A stately pleasure dome decree:*
> *Where Alph, the sacred river, ran*
> *Through caverns measureless to man*
> *Down to a sunless sea...*

These words epitomize a dream landscape wherein everything seems larger than life and twice as interesting. Coleridge said he transcribed the words exactly as they had appeared to him in his dream, but while doing so was distracted for an hour: on returning to his poem, he found that the images had melted away. For him, "there was no conscious division between day and night, between not only dreams and

intuitions, but dreams and pure reason"; in other words, he barely distinguished the difference between his waking life and the experiences of his dreams.

Robert Louis Stevenson wrote extensively about his "brownies"—little people who helped him to plot his stories in his dreams. Each night, before he retired, Stevenson would try to pick up the plot of the previous night's dream and continue the drama in his sleep. He publicly acknowledged the brownies' help, and described himself in his 1892 essay *Across the Plains* as one of the few who relied on "the harvest of their dreams" for inspiration. One of the most famous scenes in *The Strange Case of Dr Jekyll and Mr Hyde*,

__Above:__ Oberon, Titania and Puck, by William Blake, the eighteenth-century writer and artist whose dreams inspired many of his greatest works.

__Below:__ The Dream (1897) by Paul Gauguin, who spent many years in the South Sea Islands of the Pacific. His work was influenced by native traditions on magic and dreams.

Right: *Wassily Kandinsky's paintings of the* Blaue Reiter *(Blue Rider) era show the bold abstract images that this movement introduced in the early 1900s. The Russian artist defined them as "largely unconscious, spontaneous expressions of inner character." Der Blaue Reiter's yearbook had a profound influence on the nonrepresentational, dreamlike quality of modern art.*

Below: *In Raphael's* Dream of a Knight *(1505), the sleeping hero is visited by protective female figures.*

in which Hyde takes the transformative drug and changes in front of his pursuers, appeared in print exactly as Stevenson had seen it in his dream.

W.B. Yeats, whose poem "He Wishes for the Cloths of Heaven" is one of the most lyrical testimonies to the power of dreams, also claimed to have produced work based on events in his dreams:

> But I, being poor, have only my dreams;
> I have spread my dreams under your feet;
> Tread softly because you tread
>   on my dreams.

Writers including Edgar Allan Poe and Graham Greene have credited their dreams with producing some of the most successful scenes and plots in English literature, and similar examples can be found in many other languages and cultures.

Musicians have also found inspiration in their dreams. The eighteenth-century composer and violinist Giuseppe Tartini

dreamed that he had enslaved the Devil, and was astonished to hear him play "a sonata of such exquisite beauty as surpassed the boldest flights of my imagination." He tried, with only partial success, to write it down as soon as he awoke. "*The Devil's Sonata,*" he reported, "was the best I ever wrote, but far below the one I had heard in my dream."

Dreams have also inspired scientists and prompted many important discoveries. While the German chemist Friedrich Kekule (1829–96) was working on the molecular structure of benzene, he dreamed of the atoms forming long rows that fitted closely together and twisted and turned in snake-like fashion. Suddenly, one of the snakes grabbed its own tail and Kekule awoke, recognizing the symbol as the benzene ring, the solution to his problem. His lecture to his colleagues about his discovery began, "Gentlemen, let us learn to dream."

The Scottish engineer James Watt (1736–1819) had a recurring dream that he was walking through a rainstorm of heavy lead pellets. He eventually realized that if molten lead is dropped from a great height it forms spheres, and this became the basis of the invention of ball bearings.

PRECOGNITIVE DREAMS

If, as Fox Mulder alleges in "The X-Files," "A dream is an answer to a question we haven't learnt to ask," then instances of precognition—foreseeing future events—are perfectly logical. This remains one of the more controversial areas of dream research, yet there are so many anecdotal examples that it is hard to ignore the subject, or to suggest that mere coincidence is the answer. It is extremely hard to impose rigorous scientific analysis on such subjective matters as dreams, but a number of dream laboratories perform valuable studies. They are often derided by more conventional scientists, including the molecular biologist Francis Crick, who believes that the purpose of dreams is to rid the mind of unnecessary information. However, given that most people believe they simply cannot know what fate will throw at them, it is difficult to provide a rational explanation for precognitive dreams.

One theorist who tried to establish an answer was J.W. Dunne, an aeronautical engineer and the author of *An Experiment with Time.* He kept a dream diary for more than thirty years, and most of the precognitive instances he recounts are trivial—not stories worth fabricating. In 1927 he published his belief that dreams can somehow gain access to future events with the same freedom that they select episodes from the past, and he backed up his claims with elaborate theories supporting this apparent defiance of logic.

The assassinations of world leaders, major disasters and personal tragedies have been anticipated in dreams and recorded by many people *before* the real event took place. Others dream of disasters while they are happening thousands of miles away, perhaps telepathically alerted by the suffering of their fellow human beings. In 1912 a New York woman dreamed of her mother in a lifeboat so crowded it was on the verge of capsizing. Disturbed by the dream, she told her husband, who reminded her that her mother was safe in Europe. The next day, news of the sinking of the *Titanic* was published, and her mother's name was on the passenger list. Her mother survived to tell her daughter that she had been crammed, terrified, into a lifeboat, and certain of her imminent death, could think of nothing but her daughter.

Below left: Abraham Lincoln dreamt of his own death a few days before his assassination in 1865. "There seemed to be a deathlike stillness about me," he told a friend. "Before me was a catafalque, on which rested a corpse wrapped in funeral vestments. 'Who is dead in the White House?', I demanded of one of the soldiers. 'The President,' was his answer; 'he was killed by an assassin!' Then came a loud burst of grief from the crowd, which woke me from my dream. I slept no more that night; and although it was only a dream, I have been strangely troubled by it ever since." Below right: The most famous assassination of recent times was that of President John F. Kennedy on November 20, 1963. Unlike Lincoln, he did not foresee his own demise, but many others claimed that they had precognition of the event through dreams.

Above: *The sinking of the* Titanic *in 1912 was the subject of many precognitive dreams on the part of those who had friends and relatives aboard the doomed ship.*

delivered one of the first commercial aircraft, the *American Clipper*. Although Sikorsky had piloted the craft, it was not until the maiden voyage that he inspected the passenger accommodation, when he realized instantly that it was the passageway of his dream. He had had nothing to do with fitting the accommodation, and he told the story in his autobiography to explain "how a dream of early youth finally became a reality."

Another commonly reported type of premonition is a dream of someone's death, just hours or days before it happens. In many instances, skeptics argue that the dreamer may have been aware of the victim's ill health, but dreams involving people many miles away remain unexplained. Sometimes, dreamers report that a friend or relative appears in a dream to say goodbye, then discover that their visitor in sleep has, in reality, died during the night, often at the moment of the dream.

In his fascinating book *The Power of Dreams*, Brian Inglis relates the story of the celebrated Russian aeronautical engineer Igor Sikorsky, who dreamed he was walking down a narrow, bluish passageway on what at first seemed to be a ship, when he felt the sensation of flying. It was 1900, and Sikorsky was a boy of eleven: his family dismissed the dream, but Sikorsky never forgot it. In 1931 his firm

Precognitive dreams raise questions about whether we all live according to a predestined course, perhaps set by a god: to this question, there is really no answer within the scope of this book.

Right: *Many precognitive dreams feature specific landmarks like Scotland's Forth Bridge. In 1914 J.W. Dunne, who formulated the theory of serial time, dreamed that the steam train* Flying Scotsman *would crash near this bridge several months before the tragedy occurred.*

FORGOTTEN AS A DREAM

Most of our dreams are symbolic, and many theorists consider the symbols messages from our subconscious. The unconscious mind uses a language and logic of its own, utilizing images to express situations and feelings. Each symbol represents a feeling, thought, memory or mood in the dreamer's unconscious. Symbols in the unconscious reflect our emotional and intuitive world. In order to make sense of dreams, they should be recorded upon waking before the conscious mind brings more mundane matters to the fore.

Jung believed firmly that dreams should be treated as facts: one should make no assumptions except that they make their own kind of sense. He knew that they are not airy fantasies generated by the sleeping mind, stating rather that "the dream is a specific expression of the unconscious." Unlike the stories told by the conscious mind, dreams are unedited, and ordinary objects can assume monumental or threatening significance. Thoughts restrained by our conscious minds are freed and expressed in our dreams through vivid images. Jung wrote that "No dream sym-

bol can be separated from the individual who dreams it, and there is no definite or straightforward interpretation of any dream." But there are many dream symbols that recur among all humankind. Learning about their associations and meanings will enrich your dreams, and perhaps increase your emotional well-being, spiritual awareness and self-knowledge, enhancing your waking life as well.

Above: *Gauguin's* Sleeping Boy *(1881) recalls the fact that children dream vividly and remember their dreams more often than adults do, perhaps reflecting their closer ties to the unconscious.*

Left: *In his powerful surrealistic painting* The Dream *(1939), Mexican artist Ruiz combines a dreamscape with his subject's body.*

Archetypes and Emotions

Anthropologists and historians have discovered numerous features common to the dreams of everyone, irrespective of culture, upbringing or background. Carl Jung believed that "a more or less superficial layer of the unconscious is undoubtedly personal....But this personal unconscious rests upon a deeper layer, which does not derive from personal experience and is not a personal acquisition but is inborn" (*Eranos Jahrbuch*, 1934). He based his opinion on his study of religions, mythologies and folklore of many different cultures, through which he discovered that certain themes ran down the centuries, and across countries and cultures. This was the beginning of his theory of the collective unconscious. He believed that everyone inherits a myth-producing part of the mind that provides the basis for psychological life and houses the primordial images that recur in myths and legends—and dreams—all over the world. He called these universal symbols "archetypes."

An individual's psyche, according to Jung, has three levels: the collective unconscious; the personal unconscious, consisting of individual hopes, memories, etc; and the ego, or conscious mind. When the conscious mind recalls images revealed from the subconscious levels during sleep, both universal and personal meanings must be considered in order to understand their symbolic significance. This chapter explores the archetypal symbols that appear in many guises, yet have meanings common to people of all societies and personal circumstances.

According to Jung, we hide our true personalities by donning a mask, or Persona—the image that we project to the outside world. The counterpart to the Persona is the Shadow, the parts of our character that we keep hidden. The Shadow appears in our dreams, often as characters who personify negative aspects of ourselves. Also integral to the personality is the Anima (the embodiment of feminine instincts in men) or Animus (masculine attributes in women). They may appear in our dreams as powerful archetypes, which instruct us in areas that the conscious mind cannot acknowledge. Jung believed that striving to find a proper balance between the Persona and Shadow, the Anima and Animus, and the conscious and unconscious would lead to a wholeness in the human psyche, a process he called individuation. As well as these basic concepts of elements of the psyche, Jung emphasized the importance in dream interpretation of the dreamer's present circumstances (unlike Freudian analysts, who look for a full explanation in the dreamer's childhood experiences).

Opposite: Virgin and Child *by Raphael is a conventional Christian image that illustrates important dream archetypes—the nurturing Mother, with the Hero on her right and the Wise Man on her left.* ***Below:*** *A less pleasant expression lurks behind the cheery mask. In dreams, appearances are often deceptive: this dreamer may ask why he has to mask his true feelings.*

Right: Michelangelo's David is the archetypal Animus, embodying traditional heroic male characteristics.

Below: Sinister, devious and twisted, the Shadow embodies what we perceive as our worst characteristics.

THE TRIPLE PERSONALITY

Three aspects of the individual's personality appear in dreams as separate figures: the Shadow, the Anima or Animus, and the true Self. They are manifested as people the dreamer knows or recognizes, as images either real or fictitious, or occasionally in some other form. The Shadow personifies the worst faults of the dreamer, the Anima and Animus provide a balance of male and female qualities, and the true Self is the dreamer's highest potential, a properly integrated personality.

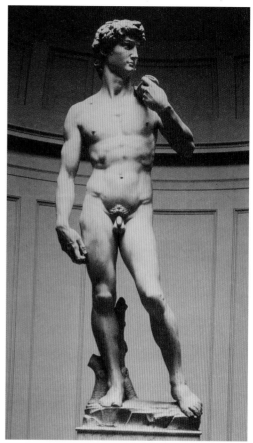

The Shadow is a mysterious, even menacing, concept, embodying all that we dislike about ourselves, or as Jung said, "the thing a person has no wish to be." It is the primitive, often brutal side of ourselves, the parts of our character and potential that are undeveloped, together with all our unrecognized frustrations. The sensitive writer may have a brutal, egotistical Shadow; the brave person, a cowardly Shadow; the generous, caring person, a selfish, twisted shadow. It is generally an aspect of ourselves that we hide from the world, and refuse to acknowledge consciously. In order to achieve a better understanding of ourselves and others, we must, however, confront our Shadows. The Shadow frequently appears while we sleep as someone we intensely dislike or envy and is usually a figure of the same sex as the person who is dreaming.

The Animus or Anima appears in dreams as a person of the opposite sex.

Anima is Latin for "soul," and in dream interpretation Anima and Animus are used as shorthand for a somewhat old-fashioned concept of masculine and feminine attributes, roughly defined as the balance between power and creativity. Everyone should try to attain an equitable balance between the emotions and rationality, and the appearance of the Anima or Animus in dreams helps to promote this. The Anima provides a pattern for "feminine" attributes in a man, and governs such characteristics as intuition, sensitivity and emotion. All the women a male dreamer has known, especially his mother, form the basis of his image of the feminine. The Anima usually appears when a man has been neglecting the "feeling" or intuitive side of his psychic life.

The Animus represents "masculine" characteristics in women, like practicality and rationality. It appears in women's dreams to encourage the development of analytical judgement and confidence in their convictions, and as with the Anima in men, it is vital to heed it. The formation of the Animus depends largely on a woman's relationship with her father, the first important male figure in her life. Dreams incorporating such phallic objects as candles or tall buildings may be abstract representations of the Animus.

The Self is a figure of the same sex as the dreamer. It is the archetype of the future personality, the figure the dreamer should strive to be, and represents potential development. Archetypal images of the Self can appear in either positive or negative forms; the negative manifestations are generally a warning that a particular characteristic is being neglected. There are four main archetypes relating to the male and female selves (although obviously male archetypes feature in women's dreams, and vice-versa), and each one is related to a function of the mind. Each has both positive and negative aspects.

Left: In a dream, the Statue of Liberty may represent a powerful Anima who provides light on the path of justice and freedom. Background: The archetypal Trickster.

25

These pages: A whole spectrum of classic female images appears here, from the perfect Mother (below) to her antithesis, Lilith, the mythical demon who attacked children (right). On the opposite page (top) are modern images of the Princess and the contemporary Amazon, a career woman. The woman below may be seen as either a seductive Siren or a confident, sexually aware Princess.

MALE AND FEMALE ARCHETYPES

Wholeness in a woman's psyche is personified by the Great Mother, or Mother Earth, a figure who incorporates the four main feminine aspects. The four characteristics influence and complement each other, as long as an equitable balance is maintained among them. The first is the Mother, representing the caring, maternal side of woman, the traditional nurturer and homemaker. This figure appears in dreams either as one's own mother, or perhaps as an older woman whom the dreamer regards as a comforting maternal figure. The negative aspect of this archetype is the Terrible Mother, a possessive, destructive, stifling figure who threatens the individual's growth and independence. The Mother archetype governs sensation.

The Princess is the second female archetype, and her province is love and rela-

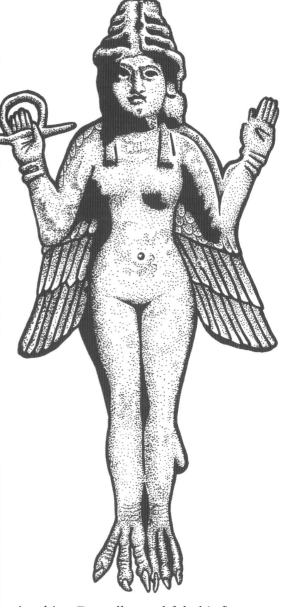

tionships. Eternally youthful, this figure incorporates the attractive qualities of spontaneity, warmth and flirtatiousness. If allowed to develop unchecked by maturity and consideration, however, the Shadow of the Princess emerges as the Siren, the unstable wrecker of relationships, doomed to flit from one unsatisfying partnership to another. In some cultures, any overt expression of female sexuality has come to be regarded as a threatening expression of the Siren. The positive female counterpart to the healthy, virile young man is the woman who is comfortable with exploring and enjoying her sexuality. Through the cultural repression of female desire,

which is an integral aspect of the Princess rather than the exclusive domain of the Siren, many women experience unnecessary and inappropriate feelings of guilt and shame in acknowledging and expressing their healthy sexual desires.

The Amazon portrays a woman's intellectual qualities. If it is a strong part of her character, she will be a career woman, competing with men on equal terms, sometimes—though not necessarily—at the expense of the mothering instinct. The Huntress, the Amazon's shadow, may be an embittered figure, and often represents frustrated ambitions. This Amazon archetype may appear in dreams as a doctor, a judge, or a lawyer.

Finally, the Priestess is the archetype governing intuition and spirituality, aspects of our personalities that are often smothered by modern life. The negative side of this is the Witch, a twisted character from the spiritual side of life. The Witch may appear in dreams as manifestations of all that is negative in womanhood, such as the bad mother, or the envious, malicious slattern.

Each of these archetypes has a male counterpart. The male Self is personified by the Wise Old Man, who often appears in

Right: *The Priestess and, above, her Shadow, the Witch.*

Below: *Masculine archetypes: the caring Father, and a police officer, an authority figure whom some dreamers identify with the repressive Ogre.*

dreams as a source of inspiration or insight. If he gives advice in a dream, it should usually be heeded. The Father is the first masculine archetype, with the Ogre as its shadow. The dreamer's own father contributes heavily to the make-up of this archetype. The Father is the embodiment of authority and justice, as well as protection. The Ogre is an oppressive figure who threatens the dreamer's individuality and appears as a menacing figure—cruel schoolmaster or corrupt policeman—against whom the dreamer is powerless.

The Youth, the male equivalent of the Princess, contains the potential for development into the Hero. Traditionally a seeker of knowledge and experience, he can deteriorate into the tramp or wastrel, forever searching and drifting.

The Hero personifies drive, ambition and daring. He often appears in dreams as a dashing, attractive figure, or sometimes as a healer. The Villain is the hero turned sour, a selfish, frustrated egotist, with aggressive instincts. When this figure appears in a dream, he represents the need to cultivate the emotional side of the psyche.

The High Priest is an elusive figure, rather like a hermit. Hard to pin down, he may be difficult to identify in dreams. He obtains

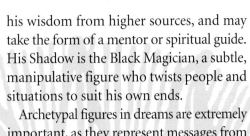

his wisdom from higher sources, and may take the form of a mentor or spiritual guide. His Shadow is the Black Magician, a subtle, manipulative figure who twists people and situations to suit his own ends.

Archetypal figures in dreams are extremely important, as they represent messages from our unconscious that are vital to the search for our true selves.

This page: Hitler, a figure from our worst nightmares, was the Villain personified. His twisted view of the world contrasts with the easy grace of the Greek Hero. *Below, left:* Mahatma Gandhi, a deeply spiritual man whose strength of will was channeled into nonviolent resistance to oppression, has inspired millions. *Background:* the sun, a masculine archetypal symbol.

This page: The appearance of dream monsters (right and below) is limited only by the imagination of the dreamer. Morgan Le Fay (below, right) exemplifies the woman whose beauty disguises an evil grasping soul. Dream monsters often represent fears that are unacknowledged in waking life.

MYTHOLOGY, FAITH AND SPIRITUALITY

Sometimes one awakens from an intense dream feeling changed, revitalized and refreshed. It is possible that the dreamer has experienced what Jung called a "great dream," one that is profoundly moving and seems laden with significance. The symbols that characterize great dreams usually bear upon the fundamentals of human existence: life and death, love, great happiness or intense depression, or life-long hopes and fears. The sleeping senses may hear unearthly music, see amazing landscapes in myriad colors and experience emotions more profound than those in "normal" dreams.

Great myths and stories are common in these dreams, which may be peopled by kings and queens, sorcerers, wizards, dragons, knights and giants, and perhaps set in enchanted places. Many involve journeys, or a quest for something that may represent an aspect of the dreamer's character. Searching for a cup or the Holy Grail, for example, is associated with a quest for love or truth, as the cup is an ancient symbol of destiny. Jung believed that myths were useful tools in understanding dreams, particularly as they encompass archetypal and universal themes from the collective unconscious.

Mythical beasts and monsters are generally interpreted as creatures fabricated in the subconscious in order to confront personal fears. They can take many forms and are often related to childhood memories of fairy tales. Their presence indicates a refusal to face up to the terrors that haunt one in waking life. Their particular significance can be identified by their most important physical and emotive characteristics within a given culture. The dragon appears in myths all over the world: the Chinese regard it as a sign of good fortune, but for Western cultures it usually represents evil. Jung considered the dragon an

important symbol representing a destructive, overbearing side of the Great Mother, who must be killed if the Hero is to be free. The unicorn traditionally represents purity, although many regard its horn as phallic, and see it as a sexual symbol. The phoenix relates to transformation and rebirth as it rises from its ashes. It signifies our need to destroy some part of our life and transform what remains into something new. Mermaids combine the symbolism of the fish (see chapter 3) with femininity to create an elusive sensuality especially fascinating to the male psyche. In some cultures, mermaids are seen as dangerous temptresses who can portend a disaster. When a woman dreams of mermaids, she may have lost touch with her creativity or repressed her sexual desires in waking life.

More than any other themes, religion and spirituality express themselves in great dreams. Throughout history, famous people have attributed their achievements to guidance and messages received in dreams: the prophet Muhammad, Joan of Arc, even Adolf Hitler. As a corporal in World War I, Hitler dreamed that he was buried under a huge mound. He awoke, walked outside,

Left: This fairy-tale castle from a medieval Book of Hours is both beautiful and impregnable. "Great" dreams are often characterized by unreal landscapes and mythical events, as seen in the stylized actions of the Hero below, left.

Below: A medieval image of Joan of Arc persuading the French dauphin to fulfill her vision and expel the English invaders from their homeland. This young peasant girl was driven by the conviction and power of her dreams to overcome huge practical and social obstacles.

Background: A Chinese dragon, symbolizing good fortune.

and seconds later his bunker was flattened by a bomb. Joan of Arc was instructed in a series of visions or dreams to encourage the vacillating dauphin to expel the English invaders from France. She led a French army herself, and her shrewdness and conviction are classic examples of a strong Animus. On the night before the Battle of Waterloo, Napoleon dreamed of a procession of figures carrying symbols of his victories, but, ominously, they were followed by gloomy individuals in chains.

Dreams of priests or holy people are almost tangible reflections of the spiritual world. The appearance of Christian saints, Hindu avatars or Buddhist boddhisattvas usually represent spiritual aspirations. Sometimes, such figures appear bathed in light, or crowned by a halo, a common symbol of divine power. They may convey an illuminating message, either about the dreamer's past or the way ahead. Angels have been recorded in dreams since Biblical times. They generally appear as intermediaries carrying a message.

Above and right:
Everyone's dreams are governed by his or her personal circumstances. The appearance in dreams of religious figures pertinent to the dreamer's faith (like the Hindu goddess, right) usually signifies a yearning for spiritual direction and guidance. Buddha received his inspiration for enlightenment in a dream, and Buddhists believe that bodhisattvas (above) postpone Nirvana in order to guide others, often through dreams. People of many faiths have received guidance from angels (far right) through both dreams and visions.
Background: *The mystical feminine image of a mermaid.*

RELATIONSHIPS AND UNIVERSAL EMOTIONS

Just as there are archetypal dreams, so there are archetypal emotions—indeed, these are far easier to recognize. Everyone lives through the same cycle of birth, life and death, experiencing a range of universal feelings, from love, elation and happiness to hate, frustration, envy and anger, and these feelings that are common to us all emerge in dreams.

Freud believed that all dreams express wish fulfillment, that they represent our deepest desires, and that in adults these desires are predominantly sexual. Obviously, sexual dreams are important, but Freud's reductionist belief was extreme. He thought that dream acts of violence, such as shooting or stabbing, are invariably associated with rape—all such acts violate the body. In Jungian dream interpretation, sex is less predominant. Violent dreams may be interpreted in a variety of ways. If we repress our sexual nature during our waking hours, it will surface in our

dreams. Straightforward dreams about intercourse often reveal the dreamer's wish for love or a close relationship, or in Jungian terms may symbolize a higher creative process. More romantic dreams of fantasy lovers may express dissatisfaction with the dreamer's real love life. Archetypal images of Princesses or Heroes are common in these dreams, as are film stars. Gushing water from a flowing tap, or a foaming bottle of champagne, may symbolize ejaculation or a new burst of creativity (which is, after all, the fundamental function of sex). The purse is a common female sexual symbol and can represent either the womb or female genitalia. It can be opened or closed, showing the female power to give or withhold sexual favors. It also represents identity.

Dreams about relationships usually refer to our real relationships; the dreaming mind rarely copies life exactly, but provides a sounding board with which to explore our circumstances. Dreams about mending objects—cars or radios, for example—often indicate a need to work at a relationship to prevent it from breaking down completely. Failure to make con-

Left: Fireworks are popular with filmmakers as representations of passionate love. While their explosions may represent sex in dreams, they may also indicate repressed anger, as seen in the phrase "there will be fireworks."

Left: Renoir's The Lovers shows a traditional image of romantic courtship. This type of dream may be simple wish-fulfillment, as both sexes act out idealized roles.

Background: A winged heart, representing love.

33

Right: A bomb with lit fuse, a symbol of mounting tension and anger.
Below: A money-driven man wheels his riches through a desert, which symbolizes an arid emotional life.

nections in dreams, such as missed telephone calls, may suggest a loss of closeness, while dreams of intense heat or cold may reflect burning passion or cold indifference toward a partner. The appearance of strangers sometimes represents one particular characteristic of a partner or relationship; by portraying an unrecognized person, the dream indicates the need for the dreamer to examine consciously this particular aspect of a very familiar person.

Anger frequently occurs in the dream world, perhaps because it is so often repressed in the conscious mind. An angry outburst can be very cathartic and is not always a negative experi-

ence. Bottled-up feelings of anger or frustration appear in dreams as contained forces on the verge of explosion: dams about to burst, or a volatile substance bursting into flames, for example. Frustration is also a common theme, frequently expressed by missing trains or planes, searching in vain for something mundane, or being unable to read an item because it is too far away. These dreams should prompt the dreamer to find the source of his real frustration, especially if they recur.

Dreams of frustration are closely related to anxiety dreams, which are often emotionally charged and fill the dreamer with nagging worry and fear. The dreamer usually feels unable to cope with the events of the dream world: he or she may stand by helplessly as friends and loved ones are injured or killed. If the dream is related to worries about responsibilities, the dreamer may be faced with a desk laden with an impossibly large amount of work, a never-ending task that he or she cannot hope to complete. Like dreams of frustration, these indicate that the dreamer should examine and confront the source of an unresolved problem in waking life, particularly if the feeling of anxiety persists after the dreamer awakens.

when we are under stress. They are the unconscious mind's way of reminding us that life isn't all bad, and they can sustain hope even in the most extreme circumstances. Survivors of Nazi concentration camps during World War II have remarked that while they were enduring some of the worst terrors ever inflicted on human beings by their fellows, their dreams were unremittingly buoyant, full of images of comfortable homes, plentiful food, sunny fields and smiling families—a complete contrast to their circumstances. Happy dreams may include symbols of good luck or peace—four-leafed clovers, doves or rainbows.

Left: This preoccupied businessman, oblivious to his personal environment, rushes to a meeting across a bridge, an important symbol of transition in dreams. **Below:** *Stress— a woman juggles domestic stability and professional success.* **Background:** *A cornucopia, symbol of abundance.*

Dreams of abandonment reflect fears experienced in childhood, when a parent's minute-long absence seemed like an eternity. This fear is manifested by images of walking through a world in which no one responds to the spoken voice, or of being surrounded by friends who suddenly vanish, leaving the dreamer alone and frightened. Alternatively, the dreamer may look in on a world or house of happy, contented people, a world from which he is excluded. If the image of a house is present, it may reflect the dreamer's inherent loneliness, as houses often represent the soul itself.

The ultimate loss—the death of a loved one—usually has a profound effect on dreams. A loved one may be seen disappearing into the distance, floating away on a boat, or departing through a gate or doorway. Dreams in which the dead person appears in happier circumstances are often a source of great comfort, and may reassure dreamers about the certainty of life after death. The death may also be portrayed more symbolically, perhaps as a house with empty or dark windows, representing the dreamer's loss.

Because dream interpretation is used most often to solve psychological problems, optimistic dreams receive less attention. Happy dreams occur at any time, and are common

People, Relationships and Activities

People in dreams fall into several categories: archetypes, which have already been discussed; the familiar faces of people we know; fictitious characters from books, films or television; or strangers. Unless the dream is a literal one, each character may represent aspects of the dreamer's own personality, or symbolize relationships with others. An unknown individual whose appearance puzzles the dreamer should rarely be interpreted at face value. Physical characteristics of the stranger may provide a clue to the meaning of the dream.

A menacing individual standing just behind the dreamer may represent his or her own Shadow; if a dreamer fights with this figure, it usually symbolizes an inner conflict. An unknown man in a woman's dream may personify her Animus. Sometimes unfamiliar people amplify one aspect of the dreamer's identity or aspirations: for example, a married couple may appear to reinforce the dreamer's unconscious feelings about marriage. People the dreamer knows well or is emotionally involved with (figures he either loves or hates), on the other hand, are often exactly what they seem. In negative contexts, such figures may express an unacknowledged negative emotion in the relationship, like guilt or fear of loss. Crowds often symbolize the forces of the unconscious. Where is the dreamer in relation to the crowd? Is he or she performing or exposed before it, or a participant? As an onlooker who perhaps feels excluded, the dreamer's insecurity is surfacing from the subconscious.

FAMILIES AND INFANTS

Family members in dreams usually represent themselves or the archetypes they have helped to create. Thus, fathers may function as authority figures, or may just be the dreamer's dad in the narrative process. The love, rivalry and struggles for independence that take place within families are often mirrored in dreams, especially when these emotions are repressed in waking life. Triangles comprise an important dream image, as this is the basic pattern of initial family relationships. A child shares its parents' love, and, according to some psychoanalysts, struggles with the same-sex parent for the attention and love of the parent of the opposite sex. Similarly, two children vie for their mother's attention and approval, a childhood experience that frequently resurfaces in adult dreams as an expression of insecurity.

Above: Shared closeness and confidence emanate from this portrait of a young couple in love.

Opposite: Encountering lifeless figures in dreams reflects feelings of alienation and an inability to communicate.

Parents are common figures in dreams. People often dream of discrediting them or rebelling against them in some way— or even of committing the ultimate act of rebellion: killing them. For good or ill, our parents are the first authority figures we encounter, and rebellion, or simply exerting our independence, is a natural part of growing up. Dreaming of killing one's parents, or of their being killed, is a vivid representation of an individual's need to end his close attachment and dependence on them. Such dreams are

most common when parents are over-bearing, either in terms of excessive authoritarian control or over-protectiveness. Likewise, the frequent appearance of family members in dreams may suggest overdependence on them.

Parents are also the first objects of a child's hero-worship; they appear as the fount of all wisdom to young children, but by the time of adolescence, the child's attitude changes, sometimes swinging erratically between extremes until the adolescent matures and the parents accept his growing independence. As Mark Twain wrote:

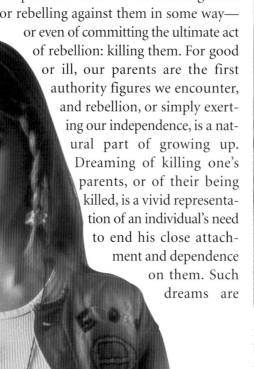

These pages: Images from family life: The rebellious teenager (opposite left and top) may appear in adult dreams as a symbol of the wish to challenge authority or to gain emotional independence from overbearing parents. Grandparents (opposite, below) appear in dreams to represent security and a sense of connectedness between generations. The devotion of a mother to her baby (left) has its concomitant in anxieties about the child's well-being and one's parental competence, which may provoke dreams related to childhood insecurities. Sometimes the appearance of a baby in dreams implies the need to nurture oneself, or a new relationship. In the dream image below, the woman is "taking control" to move away from an unhappy relationship.

"When I was a boy of fourteen, my father was so ignorant I could barely stand to have the man around. But when I got to twenty-one, I was astonished at how much the old man had learned in seven years." In dreams, parents may appear as discredited figures: a houseproud mother may become a slattern, or a respectable father a drunkard. The unconscious is revealing the dreamer's need to adopt a more detached and independent stance with regard to his or her parents.

Dreaming about grandparents or ancestors often shows concern about one's roots or background. Such dreams may also represent a sense of nostalgia for childhood: since older people usually reinforce traditional good manners and behavior, their presence in a dream provides a sense of security.

Babies represent new life, creative potential, or ideas to be developed. New parents often dream about losing their offspring and are probably expressing their anxiety about their new responsibilities through dream symbolism. New fathers commonly experience feelings of exclusion from the close bond between the mother and baby. Subconscious jealousy in this kind of tri-

angle triggers insecurity dreams that can recall childhood rivalries, losses and fears. Young mothers, on the other hand, can find a baby's total dependence overwhelming. Subconscious guilt and a desire for freedom are symbolized respectively by dream images of harming or neglecting the baby and of escaping from an imprisoned, crowded or oppressive environment to

Right and below: In dreams, babies represent new beginnings. The screaming child at right suggests distress about a new project, while the peaceful baby (far right) implies contentment and stability. The Divine Child (below) represents rebirth and perfection, the ultimate goals.

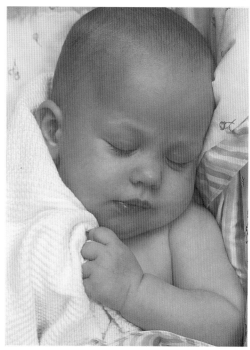

beautiful, serene and wide open spaces like beaches or mountains, or losing oneself in a crowd or anonymous place.

Dreadful things befall dream babies, whether or not the dreamer has infant offspring: they get dropped, thrown away, lost or just disappear. This may be symbolic of neglected talent or abilities. Similarly, dreams of pregnancy represent the gestation of ideas or a project. A dream of giving birth shows that ideas have reached fruition; a stillbirth may represent talents that have been ignored. Dreams about birth may also enunciate a wish for regeneration, a chance to start again, and this subject becomes more common as we get older.

The divine child is an important archetypal symbol representing perfection, rebirth and innocence. It may represent the dreamer's spiritual potential, as it has vast transforming power. Christians are advised to become "as a little child," meaning that they should cast off their worldly concerns and reclaim their trust in the essence of life. The divine child projects a similar message in our dreams. Its appearance may show how far a dreamer has strayed from his or her original aspirations.

CELEBRITIES AND PUBLIC FIGURES

Prominent people often appear as projections of the Self. Queen Elizabeth II or Winston Churchill, for example, are figures who represent steadfastness, duty and leadership. The appearance of royalty or celebrities may reflect a need for fame and recognition by one's peers. Beware of actors, however, for they are usually playing a role and are not what they seem: they may depict the dreamer, or the artificial role or stance he is adopting in life. Film stars may emerge in dreams as projections of the Anima or Animus. Dreams of

becoming a glamorous actor may simply be a wish-fulfillment device to compensate for one's own dull life, or the fact that the dreamer feels unnoticed and dowdy.

Meeting famous people in dreams may simply serve to underline the dreamer's sense of inferiority in the company of such elevated people. Many British people dream about entertaining the Queen to tea. She is a figure who seems familiar, yet her rank makes her aloof and unattainable. A dream about serving her tea may satisfy the dreamer's need to place her, or the authority she represents, under his control. The dreamer may resent the intrusion of authority into his or her life. Some analysts believe that a queen represents a mother figure and a king, a father figure.

Above and left: Celebrities often appear in dreams as manifestations of wish fulfillment. Many of us would like to be as glamorous as Marlene Dietrich *(above),* as powerful as Franklin D. Roosevelt *(top left),* or as widely respected as Sir Winston Churchill *(left).*
Background: A crown, representing royalty and pre-eminence.

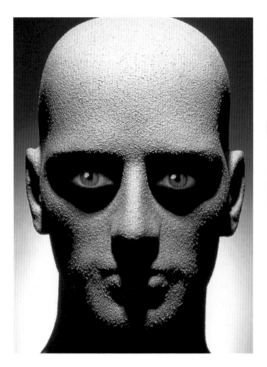

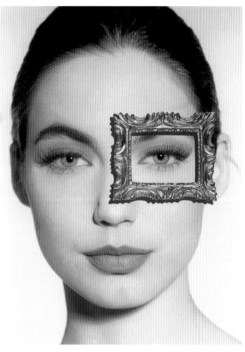

Right: *Eyes have been called the "windows of the soul" for good reason. In the image at far right, the framed left eye, associated with one's sinister side, suggests duplicity. The male figure, with its piercing eyes, has the menacing look of an automaton probing into the depths of those who have souls.*

Background: *The all-seeing eye of the Egyptian god Horus.*

THE HUMAN BODY

Feelings of vulnerability are often represented by dreams of nudity. By shedding our clothes (which represent the image we present to the world), we remove a protective shell and are exposed. If people in the dream notice and comment upon the dreamer's nudity, it may signify an area of life in which the dreamer feels at odds with those around him, or fears that he is making a fool of himself. An extreme fear of nudity may imply a dread of honesty or openness in relationships, and anxiety about exposing oneself to scrutiny from those close to us. If dream nudity goes unrecognized, it may mean that the dreamer's fears are unfounded and that he should be less self-conscious.

Sometimes nakedness can feel very liberating; casting away clothes implies the abandonment of old prejudices or practical encumbrances. It is also a flamboyant way of getting attention. The appearance of a streaker at a football match usually stops play, and certainly diverts the attention of television commentators. Dreams of streaking may express the dreamer's need for love and recognition. Nudity also conjures up images of innocence and childhood, when we could run around naked without a care in the world. Such a dream may simply be a wish to return to this innocent state.

In ancient and medieval times the body was used as a metaphor for the spiritual and religious world. It is also a valuable repository of dream symbols, especially dream puns. Feet, for example, may refer to independence, as in "standing on your own two feet"; arms may symbolize strength and protection, as in "strong right arm." Similarly, phrases like "thin-skinned," or "hard-faced" can emerge as surreal dream images. Internal organs are a particularly rich source of metaphors and images. The heart is an archetypal image of love: it is both the center of our emotional life and the life force at the center of every human being. Phrases such as "hard-hearted" or "the heart of the matter" may play a part in interpreting this image. Dreams of becoming very fat may refer to the dreamer's natural predilection for flattery; dreams of losing weight may indicate that the dreamer is being drained by the demands of others. The stomach features

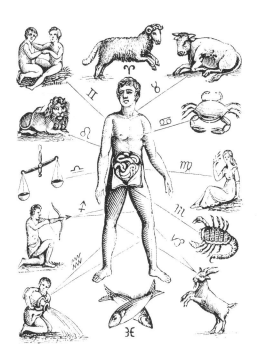

lower body relate to our instincts. Traditionally, the right side relates to morality and the left to the Shadow. Dreams may also refer to the body to provide warnings of incipient health problems. According to the *British Medical Journal*, recent research has shown that dreams may "reflect the presence of organic disease...even when the patient is unaware of it." This is not a new idea, however. The ancient Greeks and Romans firmly believed that dreams could not only diagnose illnesses, but also provide cures.

In dreams, hair may indicate strength or vanity; shaving the head represents the renunciation of worldly values and the adoption of an ascetic way of life. It may signify that the dreamer wants to strip away the extravagant trappings of his life, and concentrate on the most important areas, like family and relationships. A healthy beard represents vitality, and a white beard the wisdom of old age. Dreams of hair suddenly going white probably represent a fear of old age, or of losing one's youthful good looks.

Left: Cosmic Man, a seventeenth-century image that attributes astrological significance to parts of the body. Similarly, dreams may focus on body parts and functions, alerting the dreamer to imminent illness or imbalance. Many migraine sufferers, for example, dream of bright flashing lights several days before the onset of a headache.

in several phrases that may produce images in dreams, such as "she's got no stomach for it," "he lacks guts." "Intestinal fortitude" refers to ancient beliefs that the life force is centered in the lower abdomen.

Generally, dreams of the upper body have to do with the mental and spiritual aspects of our lives; dreams about the

Left: Frida Kahlo's painting Ford Hospital, *in which the artist depicts her own experience of dreaming of her body.*

Eyes, "the windows of the soul," may reflect the dreamer's state of mind. Bleary eyes suggest a jaded inner life. They may represent an observer, or the feeling of being watched. Seen independently of the body, an eye is the ancient symbol of the all-seeing eye of God.

Dreams of teeth falling out may make us cringe on waking up, but they often symbolize a wish to return to a time when we had no responsibilities. The loss of milk teeth is a step on the way to adulthood; dreaming of teeth falling out easily may remind the dreamer of his childhood, when his only worry was how much money the tooth fairy was going to leave behind. Teeth also fall out in old age, leaving the hackneyed image of the toothless old crone or dribbling old man. Dreams incorporating an inherent fear of losing teeth probably represent a fear of old age and loss of power. Biting or clenched teeth in dreams often express anger and aggression.

According to Freudian dream interpretation, just about any long pointed object can represent the penis, and the organ itself rarely appears in dreams. This holds valid today for people who are sexually frustrated. Since Western society is now less repressed than it was in Freud's day, more forthright sexual imagery in dreams has become increasingly common. In short, many dreamers now feel no need to hide their sexual fears and longings behind images of keys being inserted in locks or

Above and right:
Sexuality appears in dreams in many guises, from passionate lovemaking to more oblique forms like those of the orange sections (right), which resemble the female breast.

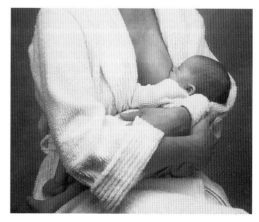

pokers into smoldering fires. The appearance of genitalia in dreams relates to sex and the dreamer's attitude to it. The phallus represents the life impulse; if a dreamer continually dreams about penises or phallic symbolism, it may be that he or she is ignoring or devaluing his or her sexuality or sex life during the waking hours.

Sexual dreams can help us to evaluate our real sex lives and perhaps improve them. Are dream lovers very different from the real partner? Are erotic dream encounters more exciting than the real thing? If so, the obvious interpretation is that the real sex life may have become boring.

Basic physical activities upon which we depend for survival often crop up in dreams. Food and eating are symbols of nurture, both physical and spiritual, and the act of eating can also have sensual overtones. Freud noted that the mouth is the first erogenous zone discovered by children, but food has been associated with sexuality for centuries.

It is important to note what the dreamer is consuming: is it normal food or perhaps a strange object, or even a person, and if so, who? Dreams of consuming someone usually represent a wish to devour them and, not surprisingly, indicate hostility. A

dream of being eaten probably reflects the dreamer's fears of being swamped by circumstances or a particular individual. Sharing a meal can be an intimate experience, and the dreamer should consider who is eating with him. Are there several people or just one? A dream of a convivial meal implies close links, and in the right circumstances, marriage. Refusal to accept food, however, implies a desire to end dependency on others, while providing a meal shows an urge to offer support and care. In Norse mythology, eating the meat of an animal or adversary means that the diner absorbs its strength.

What goes in must come out, and dreams of excreting or urinating are about letting go of waste matter that is no longer required. It can be very cathartic to rid ourselves of unwanted memories, responsibilities or experiences. Very often, however, a desperate search for a lavatory in a dream is often a subconscious expression of the dreamer's full bladder, and is the mind's way of waking the dreamer! However, an unsuccessful search for a lavatory may represent the dreamer's conflicting feelings about expressing himself in public. Finding a lavatory that lacks privacy also shows a fear of public exposure or ridicule. The inability to relieve oneself in a dream may represent the dreamer's inability to let go of certain problems or feelings. Excrement is often associated with wealth, partly because in classical literature, it was believed to contain the crude material alchemists needed to create gold from base metals.

Left: Francisco Goya's Saturn *is a nightmare image of a pitiless god consuming its offspring as a potential rival.*

Background: *The cucumber, a fertility and phallic symbol.*

Below: *The sculpture* Intoxication *portrays a state of sensual abandon that most people achieve only in their dreams.*

Right and below: The serene movement of the balloon below contrasts with the frenetic pace of the businessman driven by fluctuating stock-market prices in his quest to be "on top of the world." In dreams, flight often provides an overview of our situation, or a form of escape from the ties of everyday life.

MOTION AND STILLNESS

Dreams of running or of being chased are very common, and a classic part of anxiety dreams. Running a race usually signifies competitiveness, but the dreamer should consider his or her feelings: is there a desire to run away from something, or a fear of being left behind as contemporaries forge ahead?

At the other end of the physical spectrum are dreams of paralysis or of being rooted to the spot. Watching fire engulf a house, or the injury of loved ones while helpless to prevent it, are common anxiety dreams that indicate a conflict of emotions over a particular issue. A dreamer may long to take action in one particular area of his or her life, but is somehow unable to do so. A person torn between ambition and the attractions of a less stressful life, or someone on the

brink of a major life change, may experience this type of dream.

If dreams of paralysis are rooted in trepidation and fear of the future, dreams of flying are symptomatic of a search for spirituality and a need to get in touch with our higher selves. Expressing ambition and exhilaration, dreams of flying are a sign that the dreamer faces the future with confidence. Flying dreams may also represent escapism. The ties that hold one down are removed, and the dreamer is free to fly wherever he or she wishes. Dreams of flying in a peculiar vehicle such as a bed or a chair suggest that the dreamer's sense of adventure is tempered by a strong need for the security and familiarity of home. Flying dreams may be a simple compensation for feelings of inferiority in real life, for as Artemidorus remarked, "To fly is to be lifted above those about one." Flying is also a means of gaining an overview on life and provides an opportunity for the dreamer to assess his circumstances.

Landings are usually gentle, as the dreamer floats slowly to earth, although occasionally the exhilaration of flying can lurch into a sickening sensation of falling from a great height. Falling dreams are a sign of insecurity; falling from a high building often represents feelings of insecurity in a high-achieving world or social circle (as does balancing on a tightrope). Hitting the ground is not always the shock that the dreamer expects, perhaps showing that apparent disasters may not have long-term implications. A man who dreams of a soft landing may be expressing fears about a relationship; the landing indicates that his fears are probably unfounded and that things may turn out better than expected.

Falling in dreams does not always imply failure, nor does the dreamer always land. If he or she awakens before landing, deep-seated fears are surfacing from the subconscious. Similarly, although climbing dreams may relate to success, they often signify other desires, such as ambition and aspiration. Reaching a summit implies success, where failure to arrive at the top of a ladder usually means that the ascent represents an uphill struggle. Freud believed that climbing dreams represent a yearning for sexual fulfillment. The goal of the dreamer is an interesting factor: can the dreamer see what he or she is aiming for, or is it somehow unattainable? Such dreams may imply a need to revise our goals.

Jung regarded fights or battles in dreams as a sign of conflict between the dreamer's conscious and unconscious minds. Violence is common in dreams. If a dreamer physically harms someone, yet feels disconnected from the event, the dream violence is probably a metaphor for conflicts between feelings, ideas or decisions within the dreamer's own mind, but it can also signify frustration or hostility in a close relationship, perhaps caused by betrayal or disappointment that has not been acknowledged in waking

life. Physical aggression or dominance can also signify a desire for greater power, especially in men's dreams.

If the dreamer is the subject of violence, it may reflect a fear of assault on some important aspect of life — typically on personal relationships, professional status, health or money. Freud believed that dream violence directed toward a mother or father implied a desire to reject authority.

Dreams that are rooted in everyday activity, however bizarre the dream may present it, are the sign of a person involved in healthy communication and interaction with his or her peers. The symbolism from this area of life is usually straightforward and often depends upon puns.

Above: This woman ascending a rock face is tackling her problems (represented by the mountain) head-on. Dreams of climbing may symbolize ambition, or the sense that one's difficulties are of daunting magnitude.

Background: The ladder, symbolizing ambition or an obstacle to be overcome.

Above and right: Goitia's dreamlike Way to the Tomb *(above), with its skeletal images and jagged rocks, is a grim reminder of mortality. Cézanne's* Memento Mori *(right) recalls the practice whereby medieval monks kept a skull in their cells to remind themselves of life's brevity in the midst of their daily activities.*
Background: The skull and crossbones, symbolic of poison.

DEATH AND MORTALITY

Symbolically, death represents the end of one phase and the beginning of another. To dream of the death of a familiar figure may symbolize some sort of antagonism toward the person or what he or she represents. The dreamer's unconscious has thrown up the image of the death to provide an outlet for hostility that cannot be expressed in waking hours. Death in dreams may be associated with change, rather than with finality, or it may point to the need to come to terms with our own mortality. Dreaming of one's own death often symbolizes a desire to retreat from life and all its problems. This particular idea was expressed by the Roman philosopher Artemidorus: "To dream of death is good for those in fear, for the dead have no more fears."

There are many recorded instances of precognitive death dreams. Abraham Lincoln apparently dreamed of his own demise a few days before he was assassinated in 1865. He told a friend that he dreamed he saw a body lying in state in the White House, and when he asked who was dead, was told that it was the president, who had been assassinated. Lincoln told his friend Ward Lamont that "although it was only a dream, I have been strangely troubled by it ever since." Many analysts believe that such dreams strengthen the dreamer and prepare him or her for the oncoming crisis, be it their own death or that of a loved one. Less alarmingly, many commentators view dreams of one's death as a sign that the dreamer is about to embark on a new project or involvement, such as a job or intimate relationship.

A dream of one's own funeral may be a bizarre boost to the dreamer's ego. It is profoundly comforting to watch friends and relatives grieve over their loss, proving the depth of their regard. Such dreams may compensate for a feeling of neglect experienced in waking life: ironically, we can all be sure of being the center of attention at our funerals. A burial may represent burying feelings or traumas, or signify the end of a particular phase of the dreamer's life. Symbols of death include tombstones, skulls, scythes, and the figure of the Grim Reaper, all of which *memento mori* were common in medieval and Renaissance times.

Left: *A fifteenth-century sculpture in the* memento mori *tradition. In dreams, such images are usually classified as nightmares. However, a Chinese proverb reminds us that what is disturbing for one person may not be so for another: "The difference between a dream and a nightmare is no more than the thickness of the wing of a butterfly."*

Fauna and Flora

Nature is often present in our dream life. Natural environments, like oceans, mountains and beaches, are discussed in chapter 5. Individual natural motifs, however, are at least as common in dreams and their meanings can be highly significant, yet less readily interpreted than a general landscape in which the dreamer is obviously at ease, threatened or enchanted. Not surprisingly, perhaps, many nature symbols in dreams relate to nurturing, fertility, sex and procreation. Animals tend to stand for aspects of ourselves and those we are closely involved with, while flowers, fruit and vegetables frequently have sexual connotations. Trees have protective qualities and can signify security, endurance and permanence, while insects tend to have more negative connotations.

ANIMALS

Animals are especially powerful dream symbols and personify the instinctual side of human behavior, their attributes acting as metaphors for facets of our characters. The appearance of animals in our dreams usually implies that our basest, most fundamental instincts are emerging. Despite the restrictions imposed by the sophisticated veneer of modern life, we all have atavistic feelings within us. At best, animals may refer

to a certain animal vitality and energy; at worst, to the subconscious animalistic impulses that we try to hide during our waking life. Whether these instincts relate to the behavior of, for example, lions or mice, depends entirely upon the personality and life circumstances. At its most crude, a person who spends his waking life in an office at the mercy of a domineering boss may long for a more exciting, independent life outdoors. He or she may dream of birds soaring through the skies, particularly a predatory bird like an eagle, which represents the spirit of enthusiasm; alternatively, powerful or untamed animals may populate the dream life.

Opposite: Roses, symbols of love and feminine beauty.

Below: The lion's ferocity and strength suggests untamed passions within the dreamer.

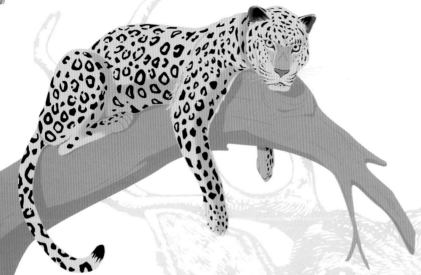

mood and the context of the dream are important. A dream about taming an animal, for example, represents a desire to restrain some aspect of oneself, or put it to constructive use. Killing an animal in a dream may deprive the dreamer of vital energies and instincts. On the other hand, if the animal personifies some dark side of the dreamer, or a fear, a dream about killing it may end the phobia or problem. Everything we do to and for animals in our dreams represents how we are treating ourselves and those around us. Such words as caging, hunting, reining, collars, feeding, clipping, branding and whipping are all associated with animals, and are used as metaphors for human behavior.

Above: In many cultures, feline creatures like this brooding leopard represent feminine attributes and are used to personify goddesses. Below: Powerful bulls in dreams may signify sexual desires. In Chinese art, the image of a man riding a bull shows the ascendancy of reason over instincts. Background: The stag is an ancient symbol of life, wisdom and virility.

In some Native American tribes, the shaman uses a power animal to act as his spiritual guide or familiar in his journeys to other worlds. Sometimes the shaman can assume the energy of his spiritual animal, using its strengths to alleviate a problem. This device is often useful in curing small children of nightmare fears: by encouraging a child frightened by dream monsters to roar or shout at them in order to scare them away, the child is empowered. More often than not, this makes the nightmares disappear.

Dream animals can be aspects of ourselves and others or represent emotions, fears or hopes. They can be tame or wild, fierce or friendly, and both the animal's

Wild animals represent power and freedom, as well as untamed instincts, especially sexuality. They may indicate a need to impose more self-discipline, to rein in wilder behavior and accept greater responsibility. Wild animals may simply be a sign of danger, their very strength epitomizing dangerous passions within us. Lions are the image of grandeur, royalty, pride and courage; watchful and intelligent, they are poised to strike at their prey, unleashing the might of their bodies in an instant. As masculine figures, they personify strength and represent the sun in many cultures. In other contexts, like all cats they are feminine and goddess symbols: Cybele, the Phrygian mother goddess, rode a chariot drawn by two lions (the Norse goddess Freya's chariot was drawn by two cats). Tigers similarly imply power (and in China, royalty and courage, qualities attributed to those born in the zodiacal year of the tiger). They also embody stealth and cruelty: not for nothing is Disney's Lion King a good guy, whereas Shere Khan in *The Jungle Book* is patently mad, bad and dangerous to know. In dreams, riding a tiger usually means danger, while paper tigers are people who seem fierce but are actually weak.

Far left: Fierce and powerful, tigers are associated with danger and stealth.

Left: A lone wolf howling at the moon is a dream image that implies raging against unalterable events and established laws. Wolves are also perceived as predatory, threatening creatures, and dreams of them may reflect a disturbance in the dreamer's sense of well-being.

Below: Horses often symbolize the dreamer's driving force or motivation. Jung connected them with the unconscious desire for the Mother.

While feline creatures appeal partly because of their feminine associations and beauty, fierce animals like bears have dual meanings in dreams. Huge, grizzly and often bad-tempered, wild bears are as far removed as possible from the image of a cuddly teddy bear. From ancient times, however, they have represented the female archetypes. The constellation Ursa Major is named for the Great She-Bear, and in cultures as distant as Eurasia and China, it was widely believed to be the throne of the queen of the heavens. In ancient Greece, child priestesses were dressed as bear cubs in the festival of Brauronian Artemis, and this spiritual association is also present in Christianity, exemplified by St. Ursula, whose name is derived from the Latin word for bear. Thus, bears usually represent mothers in dreams (who "bear" children); they depict the archetypal great mother, protecting and caring for her children. Less commonly, again because of their protective strength, they can also signify fathers.

Large, strong creatures tend to represent masculine traits in Western culture. Bulls, for example, are aggressive and can personify male sexual passion. A dream of bull fighting shows the dreamer mastering his baser instincts and represents a kind of ini-

tiation into the adult world where people are not at the mercy of their childish whims. Jung noted that "the sacrifice of the bull represents the desire for a spiritual life." In pagan societies and ancient Rome, however, bulls were sacrificed to goddesses, their blood signifying the life-blood; they are also attributes of the Hindu goddess Kali. In general, symbols of strength, power and protection imply feminine and maternal qualities in the context of cultures with strong goddess traditions, including early civilizations as well as present-day Native American and Hindu societies, while their general identification with masculine archetypes is a result of the downgrading of female archetypes and mothering roles, especially in the West.

Stags represent male sexual prowess and control. They are magnificent, proud beasts who reign over

a herd of females; solitary creatures, they are associated with the bachelor, who may be called "a bit of a stag" if he has a lot of casual relationships with girlfriends. The same criteria apply to wolves, but they also incorporate images of stealth and deception. The phrase "a wolf in sheep's clothing" conjures up feelings of fear, and a suspicion that all is not as it seems. The primal fear of the wolf lurks not so much in the anticipation of being attacked as in the drawn-out terror of being stalked and pursued by a malevolent creature. It may represent a "devouring" character like the dominant parent who cannot accept a child's maturity and continually attempts to exert an overbearing influence. As well as being aggressive and sexually predatory, the wolf sometimes stands for a more fundamentally sinister threat: the werewolf, half man, half wolf, threatens the very identity or survival of a human being.

Sometimes wolves appear in dreams in a heroic mold—a solitary figure (the lone wolf) who courageously defies hunters. The dreamer may well identify with the wolf in this instance, showing a desire to be unconventional and a wish to triumph in the face of established mores. Again, in some ancient cultures the wolf represented the mother archetype, as in the Roman concept of the she-wolf, nurturer of Romulus and Remus, the mythical founders of Rome. The identification of a dream wolf with a mother figure is, however, less common than the interpretations already mentioned.

Monkeys in dreams have complex, ambivalent associations, and the context is crucial in determining the significance for each dreamer. As homo sapien's closest genetically related animal, they can stand for intelligence (the Wise Monkeys) and community, since their family and social relationships also resemble human models. However, they also represent the archetypal trickster, as, for example, in

riding can also represent liberation or escape. The color of the horse may be important: white signifies a ride toward renewal (like the white horses of myths and fairy tales), while a black horse may be the bearer of bad news. In Freudian dream interpretation, a wild horse represents the intimidating aspect of the father figure.

Dogs—"man's best friend"—have equally close associations with humans, representing fidelity, loyalty and protection. They may appear as guide dogs in dreams, and were regarded as healers by the Celts and ancient Greeks, still a widespread association today. Many mythologies associate dogs with the underworld, or with companionship beyond the grave. Traditionally, dogs are the guardians of the underworld, Cerberus being a familiar example.

Cats are more complex creatures, and are connected with the feminine, intuitive side of our souls. Elegant and slightly mysterious, they are very personal images in dream symbolism, usually representing the Anima for men and the female archetypes for women, especially the priestess and her shadow, the witch; and the princess and her shadow, the temptress (both of whose characteristics are represented in the alluring, capable and aloof fantasy character Catwoman). Because of their "nine lives,"

Opposite page: The pinup model at top, posed with a black cat, shows the symbolic association between feminine and feline. The faithful dog (below) is an emblem of protection and fidelity. **Background:** *The pig may represent both greed and fecundity.* **Left:** *A sacred cow may appear in dreams as a pun on institutions or ideas that the dreamer wishes to challenge.* **Below:** *The gentle sheep, which becomes disoriented apart from its flock, may be either a symbol of harmlessness, or a harbinger of fears about loss of identity.*

Native American societies and in their identification with mischief, playfulness and cunning in the Western world. Like bulls, they may symbolize a regressive tendency in the dreamer's psyche.

Domestic animals do not always represent the domestic side of our natures. After all, many powerful beasts fall within this category, including horses, cows and pigs. However, in general they are more familiar and personify less strong or negative emotions, or less dangerous aspects of our characters, than wild animals. Horses, for example, are noble creatures whose association with people is timeless. They can represent the personal driving force and may appear in dreams either refusing to move, or, alternatively, running away with the rider. Dreaming of horse riding is often said to represent sexual longings in teenage girls; in adults, it may refer to the more abstract concept of the duality of our "higher" and "baser" personalities. Some interpreters regard the rider as the higher self and the horse as the lower self, symbolizing these two sides of our nature and raising questions as to which one is dominant. Horse

Above: *In Western societies, the snake is usually a sinister dream symbol, partly because of its Christian connotations as the tempter of Eve. However, in ancient Greek mythology, snakes were associated with Aesklepius, the god of healing. Thus the caduceus, representing balance restored, remains a universal symbol of medicine.* **Right:** *Traditionally, the owl embodies wisdom and knowledge. Since it can see in the dark, it represents our intuitive sense, which "sees" into the unconscious.* **Background:** *The dove with olive branch—a universal symbol of peace.*

they are associated with survival. Another particularly feminine image is the rabbit. Incredibly fertile, they are symbols of procreation, and also represent intuition, gentleness, sensitivity and compassion, the major characteristics of those born under the Chinese sign of the rabbit.

Farm animals like pigs and cows are related, not surprisingly, to food, and to sustenance in general. The pig, somewhat unfairly, has come to embody greed, gluttony, filth and bad manners, while the cow, the provider of milk, symbolizes nourishment or the mother figure and is a near universal goddess symbol. Sheep can appear singly, or in flocks (and are, of course, frequently encountered by insomniacs). A flock of sheep may signal fears about a loss of direction or identity, or the absorption of one's individuality by a greater corporate body. Artemidorus recorded a dream about sheep that shows the care he took in relating dream symbolism to personal circumstances. A man who was expecting to inherit some money dreamt he was shearing a sheep, which he left half shorn, taking away half the wool. He first interpreted it to mean that he would only get half the inheritance. In the event, the dreamer inherited nothing; Artemidorus rather pragmatically revised his earlier opinion to the effect that leaving a job half done in a dream is a bad sign.

The animal that most represents the sinister side of human behavior, with over-

tones of menacing stealth and predatory sexual activity, is the serpent, partly as a result of its cold blood and slipperiness. In Christian belief it was the first wicked animal in the Bible, and in dreams its shape has clear phallic implications. Snake dreams usually occur when the conscious mind has repressed darker, instinctual feelings, classically when a person is sexually repressed. Dreams about snakes emphasize feelings of violation, strangulation or intrusion. They can, however also represent wisdom. In mythology and art, snakes are often depicted as the guardians of secrets and temples.

BIRDS

In general, birds represent freedom, flights of fancy and spirituality, or the dreamer's aspirations, imagination and ideas. They may manifest the spirit flying toward higher, even Divine, things. In a man's dream, a bird can represent the Anima, the feminine side of his personality; for a woman, it may represent the Self, the idealized archetype of the future. White or black birds are the most common manifestations of the Anima or the Self, the black bird representing the dark, neglected side of the personality. Birds can also appear as messengers. Because they observe events from a great height, they are objective and far-sighted and in dreams can help us with decisions about the future.

Specific birds symbolize particular attributes or aspirations. Traditionally, an owl represents wisdom and the Amazon archetype, but in dreams, probably because it is a nocturnal bird, it often represents the soul of one who has died. In both ancient Egyptian and Christian cultures, it was associated with death, misfortune and spiritual darkness, but an owl in a dream is more likely to educate and guide the dreamer than to be a harbinger of doom.

Birds can also symbolize emotions or aspects of our relationships: territorial birds like blackbirds may signify jealousy, while the thieving magpie may appear as an outside threat to a relationship. The cuckoo in dreams represents usurping another or overstepping boundaries in a relationship, while the pelican and goose both stand for the more positive traits of mothering, comforting and nurturing.

Beautiful and stately, peacocks occupy an ambivalent place in dream symbolism. They can represent a beautiful or glamorous person in the imagination of the dreamer. The perfect circle of their colorful tail feathers signifies wholeness, while the many eyes can mean either vigilance or illumination (as stars in a dark sky). Proud birds, they also symbolize vanity and coquettish or ostentatious characteristics, especially in men.

Cockerels are an ancient symbol for lust. Crude, bombastic and loud, a cock can also represent arrogance or conceit, particularly in men. Chickens, on the other hand, have a more utilitarian aspect. They are flightless birds whose value lies in their eggs, symbolizing growth and hope for the future.

Doves are birds of calm and serenity, symbolizing peace in Christian cultures. In dreams they represent the Anima, conveying a message from the depths of the dreamer's being. Ravens are, in symbolic terms, the antithesis of doves. Sinister and black, in folklore they represented the Devil. In dreams ravens or crows can personify the Shadow, the dark side of our nature where we hide our blackest emotions from the world. They may also depict a sinister father figure.

The symbolism of caged birds is self-evident. A dream of a bird fluttering pathetically against the bars of its cage indicates that the dreamer feels trapped by an obstacle in his or her life. Freedom is curtailed by a barrier that restricts the potential to fly, preventing the realization of personal ambitions. Flocks of birds are usually an exhilarating image, particularly if the birds are many-colored. To dream of a flock flying upward represents some sort of transformation, or the achievement of an important goal.

The most significant mythical bird is the phoenix, which universally symbolizes renewal, revitalization and rebirth. Traditionally represented as half eagle and half pheasant, the dying phoenix builds itself a funeral pyre set alight by the sun's rays, then miraculously rises again from the ashes. The associations with the Christian belief in resurrection are obvious. In dreams, the phoenix may point toward something in daily life that needs to be changed or altered, even destroyed, and the remains metamorphosed into something fresh and new. The extinct dodo stands for something that is either lifeless or anachronistic. Both of these birds appear in dreams, though their meaning can be abstract and cryptic by comparison with other creatures.

*Above: The shadowy figure of a raven at the Tower of London. As carrion birds, ravens are often linked with death and regarded as harbingers of doom. They also personify the Shadow—that side of the psyche that conceals our darkest feelings. However, in some spheres of Native American belief, the crow or raven is the Magician who orchestrates the world, and in Japan, the bird is regarded as a divine ambassador. **Background:** The phoenix, symbol of rebirth and renewal.*

Above: The elusive fish may suggest the phrase "something fishy," meaning that a situation is not what it seems to be. A fish's appearance in dreams can reveal unease or confusion. **Background:** *The celestial starfish.* **Below:** *A dream image like Botticelli's* The Birth of Venus *represents love and beauty emerging from the unconscious.*

MARINE LIFE

If birds represent our souls and conscious aspirations, then fish, which belong to the "underworld" of water, often represent feelings deep in our unconscious, perhaps submerged emotions that we must "fish" for. In most cultures, fish symbolize the feminine qualities of intuition, fertility, creativity and inspiration. They can also represent insights into the unconscious, and fish caught in a net and brought to the surface represent the recognition of these insights by the conscious mind. A dream about dead fish floating to the surface of a murky pond indicates that the dreamer is depressed: the self-image is poor, creativity and inspiration are lacking and life seems dull or hopeless. Fish swimming against a current portray a conflict between emotions and the archetypes of the collective-unconscious level, a problem that can be resolved only by reconciling conscious needs and desires with one's personal archetypal images—recognizing both their positive and negative aspects—however hard this may seem. Failure to accept the need to resolve such profound disharmony will leave the individual feeling like "a fish out of water."

Fish are cold-blooded: the phrase "cold fish" refers to an emotionally detached or distant person and a lack of passion or empathy. Although they are phallic in shape, fish also represent impotence, because they are limp as well as cold. Being pursued by a shoal of carnivorous fish is an expression of fear that the unconscious, that repository of hidden hopes and fears, will take over, indicating that the dreamer has constructed an elaborate public persona at extreme odds with the genuine personality, and fears exposing or being overwhelmed by the true self.

The appearance of dolphins in dreams often represents a transition from sea to land (and, on gravestones, the spirit departed for the afterlife). Their symbolism is entirely positive: they indicate intelligence, happiness, friendship and spiritual enlightenment. A dream of being swallowed by a fish could indicate the need for womblike security. This is especially true of the consuming whale, a mother figure that either offers benign protection or threatens to smother the dreamer.

Crustaceans often surface in dreams from the depths of our unconscious; they are primitive forms of life and represent unformed ideas and energies. With their hard shells, they can signify emotional unavailability and unwillingness to com-

municate. The appearance of a crab, which moves sideways, may indicate skirting around a problem in waking life, rather than tackling it head on. Alternatively, a crab can stand for someone the dreamer knows, warning of a possible betrayal or underhand behavior on the part of that person. Dreaming of an oyster without its shell indicates vulnerability and the lack of defenses or strength against the hazards of the world.

Shellfish and shells often portray female genitalia because of their shape. This is particularly true of the scallop and cowrie shells, which are both ancient yoni symbols. A man who dreams of oysters or shellfish snapping at his probing stick is self-explanatory: he fears sexual rejection. If he dreams of collecting or admiring shells, his subconscious is expressing deep-seated sexual longing. Coral symbolizes the life blood, while the salt of the sea represents purification and rebirth.

INSECTS

The spider is usually a phobic symbol, and its appearance in dreams suggest unresolved anxiety. One may feel caught in a "web" of circumstances that limits choice and freedom, or threatened by an insidious force that seeks to drain one's life.

Another menacing dream insect is the scorpion, with its hidden venomous sting, which may convey unconscious feelings of danger and fear of treachery in some important relationship. Historically, the scorpion has been perceived as a symbol of hatred and envy, but it can also be an emblem of protection, since it was believed to produce

an oil that could counteract its sting.

The mercurial dragonfly may alight in one's dreams as a harbinger of instability (because of its erratic flight), or as a symbol of the longing for a summerlike state free from everyday contraints. The grasshopper and the cricket share these carefree implications, while dreams of industrious insects like bees and ants, working in harmony, may show a deep-seated need for productivity in a communal setting. Conversely, swarms of stinging bees or ants have a clear phobic connotation, as seen in certain horror stories and science-fiction movies.

Butterflies symbolize the soul and transformation or liberation from the earthly life after death. Chuang-Tzu, a Taoist sage, said that he was unsure whether he was a man who dreamed he was a butterfly, or a butterfly dreaming it was a man.

*Above: This surrealistic image of an artist and his subject watching someone flee from a spider's web may incorporate a dreamlike pun: the artist has "captured" the likeness of the sitter as the spider captures its prey, but the sitter's true identity remains a mystery. **Left:** Butterflies, which emerge from a chrysalis completely changed, stand for both transformation and transition.*

Above: Trees, the oldest living things on the planet, represent the structure of our lives and our inner selves This image of the Tree of Life shows clearly how the leaves are connected through the branches to the trunk and roots. Right: Raphael's Adam and Eve are seduced by the serpent's promise of omnipotence under the Tree of the Knowledge of Good and Evil.
Background: Acorns, the seeds of the powerful oak tree.

FLORA

Perhaps because they have the greatest longevity of the living things on our planet, trees are important symbols with universal significance. The tree of life is a seminal image, as are the family tree and the tree of knowledge. All depict both physical and spiritual growth and development. The tree as an *axis mundi* links earth and sky. All trees can symbolize endurance renewal, rebirth or immortality. A pine tree, or one that appears particularly straight and tall, may simply be a phallic symbol (as are pine cones), but evergreens in general stand for eternal life. Christmas trees, the most universal of all evergreen symbols, were first important in pagan and Norse cultures, where they were decorated in honor of the winter solstice; Christians began to adapt this tradition only in the nineteenth century. Dreaming of a Christmas tree can signify nostalgia or a need for family security, or a longing for fertility, whether in terms of pregnancy or spiritual regeneration.

Oaks can represent holiness (especially in Celtic and Norse tradition), power, thunder and lightning and the masculine qualities of strength and sexuality. The mistletoe that grows on oak (and other host trees) is a sign of fertility and its importance in Celtic ritual is today mirrored in the Christmas tradition of kissing under the mistletoe. Dreaming of vines can indicate dependency or emotional strangulation. The protective cover provided by a weeping willow or blossoming tree portrays the female characteristics of protection, nurture and shelter.

The bark of a tree is protective, and its appearance in a dream can represent the persona, or the fact that the dreamer shows a tough face to the world to protect his or her insecurities. Seeds, especially acorns, symbolize fertility, life, unrealized potential and immortality.

A dream of climbing a tree shows a desire for personal growth, a need to strive to achieve a new goal. Fallen trees in dreams may indicate a feeling of impotence or castration, or sexual frustration in women. For men, a conflict may be developed in the subconscious with the Anima. Chopping down a tree in a dream may represent failure, a deliberate end to our endeavor to achieve new things or to develop a particular side of our personality. Rooted in the soil, trees as an obstacle in dreams— like encountering a wood on a journey or a tree in the road—may signify a fear of settling down ("putting down roots") or a loss of liberty. Conversely, a tree that is continually uprooted cannot grow or bear fruit and depicts unsettled feelings of dislocation. Dreams about digging around roots are a sign of searching for something deep within the soul.

A dream of a wood or forest is usually about the people in the dreamer's life. If the trees are tall and well-spaced, this indicates well-balanced relationships. If the trees are far apart, it shows that the dreamer stands aloof from other people and should consider why such distance has been created. If the trees are overhanging, with sharp, scratchy twigs, the dream environment can indicate being overshadowed or encroached upon in a particular area of life. The condition of the leaves is important: sometimes trees in dreams appear verdant on one side and brown and dying on the other, depicting a dichotomy in one's emotional life. A part of the dreamer's psyche may be emotionally sterile or overly withdrawn.

Flowers, fruit and vegetables are usually fertility symbols, with connotations of nurturing, caring and vitality, or they are more straightforward sexual symbols because of their resemblance to male and female genitalia. Sometimes they imply the blossoming of the individual, often through a new relationship. Color is important here, as is the health of the plant. Flowers can represent hopes for the future. Giving someone a bunch of dead or dying flowers, for example, reveals a latent dislike, or even a death-wish toward the recipient. Dried flowers indicate that the dreamer is preserving his or her love life in retrospect, rather than living life to the full (or gathering rosebuds while he may). As with many other dream items, a pointed shape is a phallic symbol and a hollow, rounded bloom represents the womb or female genitalia, as depicted in the paintings of Georgia O'Keeffe and other artists.

Individual flowers have specific meanings. The lily represents innocence, mercy, hope and charity, while the rose symbolizes feminine beauty, love (especially the red rose) and, when in bud, virginity. In dreams, thorny roses can indicate an unattainable love or hostility in a relationship. The poppy stands for remembrance and death, associations solidified on the blood-soaked killing fields of World War I, but its links with both sleeping and death date back to ancient Greece, where its narcotic qualities were recognized. The chrysanthemum and lotus have the greatest symbolic resonance in the East: the former is a symbol of luck, happiness and wealth in China and Japan (where it is the national flower); and the latter is an important Hindu and Buddhist sacred flower representing purity, beauty and fertility (because it is a yoni symbol).

Fruit in general can represent work, or the development of a project that is "bearing fruit." It shows the more mature phase of a relationship or stage of life: after the blossoming of the individual comes the fruit, which is something to be savored. Apples, the fruit with which the serpent tempted Eve in the Bible, depict earthly desires and love. A dream of stealing apples implies trying to procure a love that does not rightfully belong to the dreamer. A large round fruit, such as a watermelon, represents pregnancy. Traditionally, peaches have stood for lasciviousness in the West because of their resemblance to women's breasts, while in the East, they represent paradise, fertility, marriage and immortality. From the Christian tradition, wine as the blood of Christ imbues grapes with the virtues of sacrifice and truth ("*in vino veritas*"), while they can also symbolize gluttony and overindulgence, for obvious reasons. Dreams of peaches and wine, therefore, need interpretation within a specific context: most commonly, such dreams are about sensual desires and pleasures.

*Above: When flowers appear in dreams, their color has symbolic significance. The color lilac, as seen in this still life by Van Gogh, is often associated with death and mourning. **Background:** A palm tree, whose leaves are traditional symbols of triumph. **Left:** Red is linked with both passion and remembrance, as in the case of poppies, which are an emblem of the battlefields and burial grounds of World War I.*

Structures and Buildings

Buildings of all kinds appear in dreams, including familiar ones like homes and schools, as well as fantastic or imaginary ones. A dream of the home usually refers to the self, and its rooms and interior features symbolize aspects of the personality. Other familiar structures—factories, hospitals, schools, prisons, theatres and places of worship—often stand for the dreamer's aspirations and fears, while dreams of castles, fortresses and palaces most frequently indicate archetypal and mythological themes.

HOME, SWEET HOME

Jung was the first dream analyst to define the house as the "mansion of the soul," although the metaphor had been used for centuries in Western literature. Houses usually represent the dreamer. A house is made up of a series of rooms that have independent functions, yet are linked to each other. Generally, the ground floor represents the conscious mind in dreams; the cellar or basement, the unconscious; and the higher floors, the spiritual self and aspirations. The condition of the dream building represents the outward face the dreamer presents to the world: a dilapidated exterior with broken windows and a door hanging by one hinge suggests a person with problems. The type of building—picturesque cottage, contemporary-style home or palace—has to do with the dreamer's self-image.

While Jung was working with Freud, he had a dream about a large house. He wandered around it, discovering a cellar full of prehistoric remains, a cozy living room and a panelled, rather dark, ground floor.

He related this dream to the house where he grew up. His parents were religious, with views that Jung began to reject as he learned more about comparative religion—the area of his life represented by the dark ground floor. He realized that the cellar represented his instinctive belief in the collective unconscious.

Opposite: This magnificent Thai temple, with its stepped terraces, symbolizes the ongoing ascent toward spirituality.
***Below:** The house is the symbolic "mansion of the soul."*

Above: *Bedrooms are private places where we can be ourselves. In a dream setting, Kandinsky's* Bedroom in Anmillerstrasse, *with its cluttered look, might suggest the dreamer's need to reorder his or her priorities, and perhaps clear out some "emotional baggage."*

Right: *The kitchen represents nurture, and the fact that there is no food in this refrigerator may imply a feeling of emptiness in one's inner life and a lack of resources for self-care. This dream protagonist may need to go shopping for some emotional support.*

This dream also underlined, for Jung, the vital differences between his methods of dream interpretation and those of Freud. He felt that they had grown so far apart that he did not dare tell Freud about the prehistoric bones in his dream, for fear that he would interpret them as Jung's latent wish for Freud's demise.

Dreams about one's own home, often incorporating trivial events from everyday life, are among the most common. They enable the dreamer to clarify the

events of the day, but often contain slightly inaccurate details or anomalies. The exterior may bear no resemblance to the real home, even if the interior rooms are familiar. Furniture is misplaced, appliances are the wrong size, incongruous items may appear, as well as strangers. The dreaming mind uses such details to draw attention to worries or hidden memories, or to review problems from a new angle. It is possible to interpret the dream by linking the trivial domestic details to wider archetypal and symbolic themes.

The various rooms of a house represent different aspects of our personality and life. The kitchen, where food is prepared, depicts nurture and caring both for ourselves and others. A well-stocked kitchen represents a person with the mental and emotional resources to look after him- or herself. Slaving over a hot stove in dreams, continually preparing meals for others, but with no feeling of satisfaction, can mean that caretaking of others may be diminishing the self-esteem, or even damaging the dreamer's own health. Dreams about kitchens with little or no food may indicate a need to consider physical or mental

well-being. The lack of food can signify a lack of spiritual or intellectual stimulus, and it may be time for the dreamer to go shopping for new interests.

Basements or cellars are storage places where people accumulate things that may one day be useful, or perhaps deliberately place things in order to forget about them. In dreams, the cellar represents the unconscious, where we repress embarrassing memories and secret fears we have no wish to confront. Approaching the cellar, perhaps via dank, creaky steps, dreamers often experience feelings of trepidation. The unconscious, like a cellar, is also a useful storage area for deep-seated emotions and ordinary information. On a simple level, when we need to remember a name that is elusive during the day, it can materialize after a night's sleep. The dream cellar should not be approached apprehensively; rather, it is healthy to try to confront whatever anxieties have accumulated in an effort to clear them out and acknowledge inner fears.

If cellars are about the dreamer's past and unconscious, living rooms relate to current circumstances and the conscious mind. Living rooms are public rooms used for socializing, so consider whether the dream room is comfortable and bright, or rather dark and poorly furnished. Is it a suitable place to welcome guests into? If not, why not? The condition of the living room reflects whether or not the dreamer is content with his or her life and relationships.

Windows look out onto the world and enable us to assess the state of our surroundings and the people around us. In dream symbolism, they represent the eyes, the "windows of the soul." Closed curtains or shuttered windows indicate that the dreamer has a blinkered attitude, or is inward-looking and introverted. On the other hand, peering into the windows of another house may indicate that the dreamer is substituting a curiosity about

the lives of others for a healthy examination of his or her own psyche. It is worth noticing whether the view is sunny and attractive or cold and bleak, as this often reflects the dreamer's attitude to life. Dreaming of opening windows may symbolize the dreamer's desire to socialize or widen his or her horizons, to hear the opinions of outsiders who could provide "a breath of fresh air." Freud believed that windows were female sexual symbols and regarded looking through the windows of another house in dreams as voyeurism.

Staircases provide access to upper floors, and in dreams climbing stairs can symbolize an emotional or spiritual quest. Descending a staircase signifies an attempt to explore the instincts and the unconscious. Details of which rooms are linked by the dream staircase and whether the journey is straightforward may symbolize the ease or difficulty involved in achieving personal aspirations.

Attics are the uppermost rooms in houses. Repositories of unused items, they house old papers, possessions and mementoes, and often symbolize childhood in dreams. As the highest point of the house, the attic looks out onto the skies and may symbolize our higher aspirations, which can be achieved only by climbing up to them.

Left: Surrounded by Christmas lights, this cat in the window conveys a sense of domestic comfort and tranquillity. Dream windows like this give access to feelings about our environment or life circumstances. Peering into a window suggests that one wishes to gain insight into the thoughts or feelings of another. A windowless "dream house" indicates an introverted personality, while open windows suggest a healthy desire to share opinions and feelings with others.

Background: Opened curtains indicate a willingness to explore the outside world and expand one's horizons.

Right: Bathrooms connote privacy and, in dreams, may serve as the setting in which we face our true selves. Here, the unconscious, symbolized by water, can flow freely.

Below: This Egyptian courtyard, a green oasis enclosed in a marble hall, is an intimate place in the midst of a public area, perhaps symbolizing the dreamer's sense of being centered in his true self while interacting with the world around him.

Bathrooms are places of purification and purging, where we go to wash off the grime of the day and relieve ourselves. Water is obviously an important element here, and in dreams often represents the life force or the subconscious. Relaxing in a bath in dreams is pleasurable and recalls the security of the womb. The symbolism of washing away our sins or wiping ourselves clean to expunge our guilt is strong, and has its roots in Christian theology. Dreams about a flood in the bathroom represent sentiment overwhelming the dreamer, and signify a lack of emotional control. Privacy is also important: dreaming about using a lavatory or bathroom without a door or in a public place indicates that the dreamer feels vulnerable and threatened. He or she needs to be unburdened of problems, but is unable to take control of the situation.

Gardens are for recreation and reflection, places to relax and unwind. In dreams they represent the inner life of the individual, and aspects of the personality that he or she is cultivating or nurturing. The colors of flowers may provide a clue as to the dreamer's state of mind, and a neglected weedy garden may symbolize the dreamer's disappointments. An excessively tidy garden with little or nothing growing may be a sign that the dreamer's emotional life is sterile. Dreams of a large formal garden may simply be wish fulfillment, but pay attention to the shapes of the flowerbeds and the layout, as their regular patterns may be important. Many people cultivate a secret garden in their dreams, using it as a private place in which to review their lives and recharge their batteries. A walled garden may reflect an excessive need for privacy—perhaps the dreamer is shutting out those who are nearest, especially if they are too close or dependent. Gardens are wonderful places to rest for a while, but they are no substitute for the love of friends and family.

PUBLIC BUILDINGS

Churches, temples and other religious sanctuaries represent a dreamer's spiritual nature, and are ideal places for meditation and reflection. They may represent a dreamer's idealism about someone or a particular situation, or may be a sign that more attention should be paid to spiritual priorities. Churches and temples are also about ritual, which can be comforting or threatening, depending upon one's outlook. A series of dreams about religious structures may be a sign that the dreamer seeks guidance from a source of higher wisdom. If the dreamer feels uneasy or like a stranger in the church, he or she should consider devoting more time to the inner life and developing personal spirituality.

Medieval European churches are often supported by flying buttresses, or adjoined by archways and cloisters. The columns and arches are important archetypal shapes and are significant in dreams. As doorways, and especially in the context of a church, they provide entrances to changed or higher levels of consciousness. Likewise, the globes, points and towers of other religious architecture may have dream meanings related to the symbolism of their shapes.

Graveyards and cemeteries often have sinister connotations, but they rarely appear in dreams as an intimation of impending death. They may simply indicate the need to think about the past. They are also peaceful places and may reflect the dreamer's need for quiet, or perhaps a chance to bury a problem or relationship or to accept changes that have taken place in life.

Castles and fortresses suggest security, but their very strength is their isolation from the surrounding hinterland, and their appearance in dreams may be a warning against becoming cut off from the people who are closest. On the other hand, the dreamer may feel the need for protection against hostile forces. In Freudian terminology, castles represent women at their most unattainable. A man's dream about besieging a castle may symbolize his lack of sexual confidence or a wishful attempt at sexual conquest of a woman who, in real life, has shown no interest in the dreamer.

Places of work, such as factories, shops and offices, are often impersonal, but in dreams they may refer to a particular aspect of the dreamer's character. Factories, where items are manufactured, may relate to the creative side of the personality. On the other hand, they are often relentlessly grim places where people are expected to work like automata. A dream of working on a mechanical factory production line may symbolize fears about the loss of individual identity: the dreamer dreads becoming a cog in a machine and feels that he or she has no individual worth.

While libraries are linked to the intellect and learning, museums represent the past. Both these images are also about memories. Books represent wisdom, or a record of the dreamer's life. A library contains ideas, and is a source of almost unlimited knowledge. Dreaming of interruption while reading or studying at a computer may represent the dreamer's inabil-

Above and left: *In Freudian terms, towers are simply phallic symbols, but they have wider implications. De Chirico's Great Tower (above), surrounded by pillars, may symbolize someone perceived as a "tower of strength," who stands out from the crowd. Dreams of a church (left) usually represent spirituality, with the tower emphasizing the dreamer's aspirations toward a higher form of consciousness.*

Background: *A gargoyle can appear as a grotesque adornment to a dream church, indicating unease in the spiritual life.*

Above: Dreams of imprisonment usually signal anxiety and frustration. For some, however, incarceration may imply relief from everyday responsibilities and the difficulty of making choices.

Below: Crucial to the formation of our adult selves, schools may appear in dreams either as nostalgic reminders of our youth, or as an impetus to continued growth and learning from our life experience.

ity to concentrate. Law courts symbolize the dreamer's discrimination and powers of judgement, or, in the case of someone who has broken the law, a fear of being brought to justice.

Hospital dreams can emerge from an excessive fear of illness, or neglect of oneself or friends and relatives. They often represent a deep need to be loved and perhaps a wish to abandon all responsibilities while someone else makes the decisions about life. Many people feel secure in the care of medical professionals, trusting them to restore their physical health. The context of hospital dreams is obviously important. Some dreamers may see themselves as heroic doctors battling to save the lives of others. This type of wish-fulfillment dream is very common.

Hotels are linked in symbolic terms to hospitals in many ways. In both places we surrender control over our care to others, so in dreams both represent places of nurture and pampering. Hotels can also be rather impersonal, even intimidating (as epitomized by The Eagles' popular song, "Hotel California"). Hotels are associated with travelling and may symbolize transition and restlessness in relationships.

To dream of being imprisoned—the extreme of institutionalization and lack of self-determination—indicates excessive demands made on the dreamer by others, especially by dependent or controlling family members or overbearing employers. Alternatively, suppressing one's own fears of emotional needs can lead to such dreams. For some, dreams of being incarcerated are not confining but are calming experiences—freedom has been given up willingly because the dreamer's responsibilities in life are too burdensome.

Schools appear frequently in dreams, probably because they play such an important part in our formative years. School dreams may be purely nostalgic, reminding us of the innocence and freedom of youth. A dream in which the school is empty or dilapidated suggests that we have unhappy memories, or still hold on to disappointed childhood expec-

tations. It may be a reminder to look forward, rather than dwelling in the past and yearning after things we can never change. Classrooms are about learning, but they are also places of intense academic and social competition, where children first learn about public esteem or derision. Dreaming about returning to the classroom of one's youth only to find that one is demoted to a lower class, humiliated before peers or stripped of some privilege reflects unresolved childhood insecurities. Such dreams are extremely common and if they recur, the adult dreamer may have a fear of his or her archetypal shadows becoming apparent.

Shops also play an important part in everyday life. In dreams they are symbolic of opportunity and reward, and our ability to seize our chances, which is often symbolized by the amount of money we have available in our dreams. Shops provide a host of dream metaphors for tackling life's problems or capitalizing on events. A bustling mall full of attractive shops signifies a life of opportunity; the dreamer can choose which shops to patronize and assess what life has to offer. A dream of standing in front of a shop window full of desirable but unattainable items represents the dreamer's feelings of exclusion from the luxuries of life. The dream may be suggesting that he or she look elsewhere for satisfaction.

The style of the buildings in a dream has a profound effect on its atmosphere. An urban landscape of skyscrapers may feel intimidating, while an office with endless rows of desks and computer terminals raises questions about loss of identity. Dream cities symbolize the community, and the dreamer's whereabouts and attitude to the dream city reflect his or her position and relationship with peers. A dream of a fantastic ethereal city may reflect the high ideals the dreamer ascribes to his or her colleagues and friends. Such

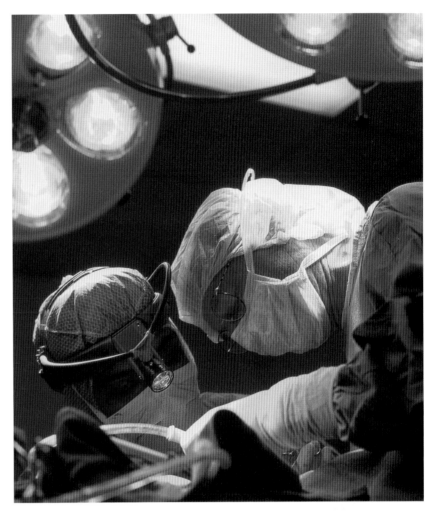

idealism may be hard for them to live up to, and the very unreality of this dream city should make the dreamer consider whether too much is expected of his or her family or peers. Dreaming of circling a city which is clearly visible but unreachable may symbolize a dreamer's feelings of exclusion and loneliness. Similarly, a town with empty streets and deserted shops may signify rejection or a fear of abandonment. Shadowy houses reflect the dreamer's lack of understanding and empathy with others, or even a lack of self-knowledge. A crumbling, ruined city may emphasize neglected relationships, but it also suggests that restoration work can be carried out to improve them. A futuristic cityscape is a sign of optimism—the dreamer looks to the future in happy anticipation, rather than dwelling on the past.

Above: Dreams of hospitals and operations may simply reflect the dreamer's fears about his or her health, or that of a loved one. If one dreams of being a skillful life-saving surgeon, it may be a form of wish-fulfillment, reflecting the need for recognition and effectiveness in waking life.

Background: A tall church tower can represent the dreamer's lofty spiritual ideals.

Landscapes and Surroundings

The environment of a dream is always important: the landscape or surroundings contribute to the atmosphere and reveal aspects of the inner life. Familiar places that appear in our dreams usually carry with them memories of the feelings we associate with them. Thus, for example, someone who was unhappy at a repressive boarding school may dream of that place when feeling threatened by outside pressures to conform at work in later life. Sometimes, the dream landscape may appear completely unfamiliar, but the dreamer looks on with feelings of loss and regret. This situation may symbolize the dreamer's underlying feelings that he or she is not ready for change and the adoption of a new lifestyle. Alternatively, feelings of elation in unfamiliar surroundings suggest that the dreamer is ready to grasp new opportunities.

Imaginary surroundings can take on any guise the dreamer brings to them, and their basic elements provide clues to their meaning. Ancient and medieval astrologers and philosophers used the four elements to symbolize the four basic characteristics of human beings: fire for passion and ambition; water for creativity and imagination; earth for reliability and fertility; and air for spirituality and intelligence. The four elements assume many different forms in dreams: water can appear as a stormy sea or a leaking pipe; air is felt as a violent, stormy wind or seen as a clear blue sky; fire may be spitting from a volcano or warming a cozy room; flowers may be sprouting from a fertile soil, or the dreamer may encounter an arid desert.

WATER

Water is a life force, cleansing, purifying and rehydrating all living things. In dreams it represents the unconscious and relates to emotions and sensuality. An anxiety dream about being engulfed by water perhaps represents a metaphorical fear of drowning, giving way to emotions that stifle rational thought or experiencing a breakdown. Jung believed that turning to face the sea in a

Opposite: Van Gogh's Autumn *in which the tall trees dwarf the human figure.* **Below:** *A diver plunges into the water that represents both the life-force and the unconscious.* **Background:** *A medieval sea monster: danger lurking in the depths.*

Right: Dreams of gazing into water may indicate the dreamer's need to plumb the unconscious mind. One may, like the legendary Psyche, see one's own reflection, or another face in the waters. In either case, they are aspects of the dreamer.

dream meant that the dreamer was prepared to confront his or her unconscious mind. He saw creatures emerging from the deep as powerful archetypal forces that conveyed important messages from the unconscious mind. Threatening sea creatures recur in the Bible (especially the Old Testament) as metaphors for evil. Freud regarded the sea and the incoming tide as elemental symbols of sexual union. A dream about swimming suggests that the dreamer should explore his or her unconscious, imagination, or creative forces. An enjoyable swim in a clear blue sea implies that the dreamer is working in harmony with the imagination; struggling against a strong current, or having trouble staying afloat, may be a warning to proceed with caution (a similar, but milder, signal than fish struggling against a current: see chapter 3). Diving represents plunging down into the mind, perhaps in search of childhood memories. The condition of the water—stagnant, muddy, clear, or fast-flowing—is a good indication of the state of the dreamer's emotions.

Water springs out of the earth in small streams, which symbolize the source of life. Seas and oceans are vast, deep voids, where all creatures had their origin; deep seas in dreams are the unconscious, home

to all our secret hopes and fears. A contrast between deep and shallow water symbolizes the differences between what is important or profound, and what is superficial. There are various ways to control water, such as dams, valves and locks. In dreams exerting control over a powerful water force represents a bottling up of emotions, a repression of feelings and instincts. What happens when water bursts out and floods the house, or a valley? Is the dreamer drowned, or does he or she float unharmed to the surface? A dream like this may encourage the dreamer to direct his or her rational side to work in harmony with instincts and feelings, instead of being ruled entirely by the intellect. Dreams of floods may reflect an incipient need for change. A person in middle age may dream of floods, symbolizing the need to adapt either lifestyle or ideas simply to keep up with others and changing situations. Suddenly aware that life is slipping by, after years of conformity, he or she may at last decide to pursue suppressed desires and goals. If he or she does not alter waking-life behavior, routines and patterns will sweep away the true self.

Sometimes the dream forces of nature, as in waking life, simply take over. One is helpless against the dangers unleashed by a powerful storm: whole communities are wiped out by a tidal wave, or flooded by

Below: In Renoir's Skiff, *two young women enjoy boating in calm waters on a fine summer's day. This dreamlike image implies that the rower feels secure in guiding her vessel on the river of life.*

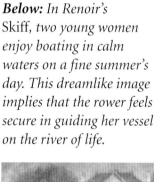

the incoming sea crashing through storm defenses. Boats can be pummelled on a storm-tossed ocean. These dreams are about conflict. The dreamer feels overwhelmed by the powerful forces of the unconscious, which may contain feelings or memories that he or she does not want to confront and which are struggling to rise to the surface. Storms may also reflect "stormy" emotions and outbursts of anger or frustration.

Recently, I dreamed I was on a ferry crossing the English Channel with my husband and a friend. We were all enjoying a conversation, when suddenly I noticed that the sea had reached the level of the deck. I was not in the least alarmed, even as the water gradually rose higher. The sea became rougher and waves swept over us, but we carried on laughing and joking in a manner epitomized by the British in adversity. My friend disappeared under a wave, but continued talking. As a wave engulfed me, I felt perfectly calm and unworried, wondering fleetingly about my small daughter below decks. Rather like a film, the dream then cut to the shore. I saw several old-fashioned Victorian lifeboats, powered by oars, bringing the survivors of the shipwreck ashore, and felt vast relief as I saw my family and myself walking down the gangplank.

It was a hugely entertaining dream, particularly when part of me was watching events in which another part of me was involved. It seems to have been a dream of reassurance in many senses. The engulfing water represented the unconscious, which held no fears for me. Perhaps it was suggesting that there is nothing to fear in surrendering to the unconscious and indulging in more introspection than usual.

Dreams about water also indicate that the dreamer will survive emotional upheavals. In many ways, dreams that force a turbulent confrontation with unwelcome feelings are far more healthy than dreams of ice, which generally symbolize a frozen soul lacking any feeling. The appearance of rain in dreams indicates refreshment after an arid emotional period, probably devoid of love and attention. It symbolizes a renewal of intellectual or emotional life.

Rivers suggest destiny, or the dreamer's emotional journey through life, and the condition of the river—cloudy, blocked with weeds and detritus, sluggish or fast-flowing—indicates the ease with which the dreamer copes with the twists and turns of life. The appearance of a canal suggests that the dreamer's emotions are strictly controlled and that they should be freed. Rivers are also barriers that have to be crossed, and can sometimes represent an obstacle in relationships. A dream featuring a river with no means of crossing to the far side may indicate that the dreamer is unable or unwilling to reach out and commit himself or herself to a relationship; to bridge the gap to the object of his or her desire seems too great a risk. Springs and water sources

Background: A ship provides security on a journey through emotional waters.

Below: A woman meditating on the beach embodies the process whereby the unconscious merges with the waking mind. Just as the tide periodically sweeps the beach clean, or brings up material from the sea, so the unconscious works to refresh and inspire the dreamer.

Right: Dream landscapes reflect the dreamer's feelings of security or anxiety. A small copse of trees may suggest either a resting place, or a block to the dreamer's progress.

indicate creativity and new ideas; for women, dreams featuring springs may be related to pregnancy and childbirth.

Encountering one's reflection in a pool of water in a dream may be a confrontation with the Shadow. An unflattering reflection may appear, symbolizing whatever the dreamer considers his or her worst aspects. Sometimes aquatic creatures like fish or even mermaids may appear to lure the dreamer into the realms of emotion and imagination, away from the cold reality of the intellect alone.

On beaches, water meets the land. A dream about emerging from sea onto land may be about birth, when we emerged from the watery cocoon of the womb to the harsh, sometimes arid surroundings of life. Beaches can also be about romantic getaways, childhood memories and happiness. Frequently washed clean by the tide, they can be seen as places of regeneration, where there is always a chance to start anew. Many people dream of escaping to an isolated desert island, which is reached by crossing water. Such islands are refuges that symbolize either paradise or imprisonment, depending on whether the dreamer wants to enjoy the island's privacy or escape it. In order to reach or leave islands, one must face and overcome the problems hidden deep in the unconscious mind (represented by the surrounding body of water).

EARTHLY ENVIRONMENTS

The earth represents stability, strength and permanence. Mother Earth is a powerful archetype suggesting familiarity, nurture, home and safety. The soil itself is a fertil-

Below: A mountain, too, may be seen either as an obstacle, or, in a more positive light, as a challenge.

ity symbol; it nurtures plants and allows them to grow. Dreams of digging or turning the earth refer to one's creative side, the part of the mind where ideas are planted and projects take root. The earth appears most obviously as landscape: mountains signify peace or obstacles; valleys, security; deserts, emotional or spiritual drought; forests, darkness and danger, protection or the unconscious; and countryside, peace and freedom. To dream of sitting or lying on the ground shows a desire to remain rooted in reality and not to take off on wildly adventurous activities or flights of fancy.

Manmade surroundings such as cities, as mentioned in chapter 4, take on the relevance we endow them with in everyday life. Towns and cities represent the community and the dreamer's position within it, as well as his or her relationship to it. They encompass everyday relationships with family and friends and the responsibilities of life. A ruined city, for example, may indicate that the dreamer has been neglecting significant relationships or ideals. A bustling town with friendly cafes, open-fronted shops and clean streets represents a healthy social life and warm relationships. A large city characterized by impersonal tower blocks and buildings suggests that the dreamer has many acquaintances but few close friends. A walled city suggests a need to protect one's friends and family, or hints at a feeling of exclusiveness and a desire to keep interlopers at bay. The dreamer may be in danger of becoming cut off from new outside influences.

The dreamscape reflects the dreamer's feelings, particularly concerning security. Meadows and fields traditionally indicate one's present situation. A downward slope to the left indicates a leaning to the logical; to the right, a stronger intuitive side. An uphill slope to the left shows that the dreamer may have problems with the logical, rational side of life, and similarly, a

right-hand uphill slope indicates difficulties with expressing emotions. If one's dreamscapes repeatedly contain craggy, snow-capped mountains, this probably reflects on relationships with others as well as the emotional life: the snow indicates a cool inner life and the mountains, a certain aloofness. Perhaps the dreamer is holding back from something or someone. If he or she wants to climb the mountains, curiosity, ambition or a desire for new relationships are likely to be indicated by the perceived challenge.

THE ELEMENTS

Air, the element that symbolizes otherworldliness, is equated with wisdom, spirituality and the higher self. A gentle breeze represents the spirit, either the dreamer's, or that of the life force (often called the Holy or Great Spirit). Dreamers may find themselves floating on a cloud through clear skies, or travelling in a hot-air balloon. Floating through the air enables the dreamer to gain an overview of life. It is also a way of indulging in imaginative fan-

Above: The presence of the angel in Savaldd's Tobias and the Angel *brings paradise to earth. Dream landscapes are limited only by the dreamer's imagination, and when they assume mythical proportions, the dream is deeply meaningful. Some analysts call these "great dreams," which have profound effects on one's life.*

Background: An urban skyline, symbolizing either alienation or optimism for the future.

Right: Rough Sea, *by Monet, lends itself to dream analysis as the sign of a troubled mind.* **Below:** *Dream rainbows have connotations of hopefulness and good fortune to come.* **Below, right:** *This grim industrial dreamscape suggests a personality with a regimented waking life who is out of touch with his or her spiritual needs. The chimneys represent a latent desire for spiritual awakening, but the upward way is obscured by polluted smoke.*

tasies, although the dream may incorporate a warning about flying too far and losing touch with reality. Stronger winds can be a sign of transformation, as in the phrase "wind of change." In dreams, one may float contentedly or be blown with some force by a stormy wind. Floating implies a lack of awareness of, or deliberate control over, one's direction, but a dream of being buffeted to and fro indicates a fear of surrendering oneself to spiritual forces that are too powerful for conscious control. Stormy winds and hurricanes are destructive and can be a sign of anger or conflict between one's rational self and religious or spiritual needs. A breeze blowing over water stirs it and in dreams represents a new life, or an idea forming in the dreamer's unconscious. Messages are also carried in the wind or on the "airwaves"; the sound of the wind in dreams may communicate either benign or threatening change.

Rainbows, a combination of air and water, arch over land, inspiring feelings of optimism and happiness. In the Old Testament, the rainbow was a sign of the covenant between God and man, and in most faiths it symbolizes a link from earth

to a higher or divine plane. Legend has it that there is a pot of gold at the end of the rainbow, and the appearance of a rainbow is auspicious in most cultures; in dreams, it is a universal symbol of hope and good luck. The spectrum of colors is produced by light passing through water droplets, creating an arc of color that symbolizes good fortune and healthy relationships. Fog, a more gloomy combination of elements, indicates doubt and uncertainty in the dreamer's life. The way ahead is unclear; goals are hidden and emotions confused. The appearance of fog in a dream may indicate a need for a change of direction in the life of the dreamer, or an alteration in circumstances that seems confusing at first. When fog lifts in a dream and is replaced by sunlight, the sun illuminates and clarifies one's situation, indicating that a change in life has been accepted after initial doubts, or uncertainty resolved. Fog should not be confused with smoke, which is equally obscuring, but can also stifle and choke.

Lightning is a powerful natural force that provides a sudden clarifying flash of illumination and is associated with intuition or messages from a deity. In dreams, it acts as a revelation, providing awareness and inspiration. It can also transfigure creatures, people or situations. As an uncontrollable force of nature, potentially destructive, it implies that there are powers beyond the dreamer's control that must be taken into account. It is also a common masculine motif and can represent the archetypal hero or villain.

Lightning can start fires, and fire is another transforming force. It alters everything it touches, and its energy signifies change, destruction and purification in dreams. It is interesting to note that while fire is the symbol of life and passion, nothing can actually live in it. A dream fire that burns wildly out of control symbolizes overwhelming passions and feelings. The

dreamer may be terrified by their very strength and power. The dream may urge him or her to take control of feelings or ambitions by fighting the fire. Roaring flames may also symbolize anger toward something or someone. A fire blazing in a hearth evokes a very different reaction, symbolizing domesticity, comfort and companionship. If the emphasis is more on the light of the fire, rather than the heat and potential threat from the flames, fire may symbolize the enlightened spirit, or the Self. The appearance of fire in dreams usually signifies extra energy or change.

Above: *The cypress in Van Gogh's* Starry Night *thrusts toward a swirling, transcendent sky to which the people in the sleeping town below are oblivious.* **Below:** *This image, with storm clouds gathering on the horizon, suggests that the dreamer's hopes for steady progress may be impeded.* **Background:** *Fire, a consuming elemental force.*

NATURAL CYCLES

Change, mutability and the unending cycle of life are often symbolized by the weather and the seasons, which provide many metaphors easily translated by the dreaming mind. A dream that progresses through the seasons from autumn to summer may signify an inner transformation. Dreams of moving from summer back to winter, however, suggest that the dreamer needs to recuperate and recharge his or her spiritual batteries. Retrograde motion of the seasons implies the need to adjust daily routines to accord with the "natural order" of things, or the dictates of unacknowledged subconscious forces.

Spring provides a new warmth: the sun reappears and the days get longer, bringing about rebirth. Summer is a time of consolidation, luxuriant growth and enjoyment of life. In autumn we harvest the fruits of our labors, reflecting on the works of the seasons past. During winter we retreat inside while the ground is unyielding and cold. In dreams, spring often represents childhood; summer, youth; autumn, maturity, when the individual's life should bear

fruit; and winter, old age. A dream about summer following winter may symbolize convictions about life after death.

The sun itself is a powerful symbol crucial to the folklore and religions of many cultures. Bright and powerful, it often represents the intellect and intelligence—an object illuminated by sunlight may be a source of inspiration in dreams. The sun

Above, right: The eternal Child, here surrounded by flowers in an alpine spring scene, is a sign of optimism about the future. ***Right:*** *Kandinsky's* Winter I, *a bleak, forbidding image, imparts a sense of isolation with its narrow shuttered house in the background, bare trees and impending snow and ice.* ***Background:*** *The sower, replenishing the earth with seed.*

his intuitive side, and he may fear surrendering his rational self to the more subtle and less quantifiable forces of the unconscious. Some people, however, find the peace of the evening very soothing, and this type of dream atmosphere suggests that the dreamer has a healthy and contemplative inner life.

Day or night, dawn or dusk, all have a profound influence on the atmosphere and meaning of a dream, simply because our behavior patterns are tied to the passage of the hours. The time of day in a dream may relate to the dreamer's age. If dawn represents potential progress and youth, high noon stands for maturity, and dusk for the decline of creative powers, especially in old age.

Left, below and background: *The sun and moon, constants in the dreams of humankind, are universal symbols. The morning sun pierces the gloom of the forest (left), heralding a new day. The full moon shining on the darkened sea (below) symbolizes a calm, untroubled soul, as expressed in the Zen Buddhist aphorism "Mind like water, mind like moon."*

is considered to embody masculine energies, and Artemidorus generally regarded its appearance as a good thing, "except for those who want to keep something secret or hid." A dread of sunlight may be related to the dreamer's fear of the truth becoming known. Sunrises symbolize new beginnings and revelations, as in "suddenly it dawned on me."

The sun illuminates our world by day, and its opposite, the moon, shines through the night, representing in dreams the intuitive illumination of the unconscious. It belongs to the realm of the feminine and the unconscious soul, and can symbolize spiritual wisdom and the imagination. Dreams of flying to the moon, or metaphorically "wanting the moon" are about desire and trying to obtain the unattainable. A full moon may signify serenity and calm, emphasizing the dreamer's contemplative nature, while a new moon represents new beginnings and projects. The darkness of night is itself a powerful conveyor of mood and suggests that the dream is about the unconscious. Shadows can appear menacing, and dreamers may fear what is about to leap out from the dark: the dreamer's intellect seeks to overpower

Passages and Transitions

Life around us is constantly changing. Time does not stand still, and we are presented with new challenges and situations, whether we embrace them willingly or resist them. Although people commonly imagine that they are stuck in a rut, even in relatively featureless periods of life, attitudes and preferences alter in the course of trying to accomplish ambitions and goals, however modest they may be. During sleep, events are sorted in the unconscious, which reminds the dreamer of the journey through life and the inevitability and, in many cases, desirability, of change. Journeys are common dream subjects and often reflect the ease with which the dreamer adapts to shifting circumstances and relationships. Freud regarded all journeys as reminders of death, and if a sense of departure occurs in a dream, it may symbolize some aspect of one's own death or the loss of a loved one.

If a dreamer has recently experienced a major life-changing event such as a bereavement, marriage or childbirth, his or her dreams are often full of comforting images of familiar surroundings and the old way of life. The unconscious restores a balance between the strangeness of the new lifestyle and the continuity with earlier patterns, in order to help an individual to accept change. On the other hand, a dull waking life often promotes wishful dreams about new relationships, danger, challenges or such excitement as exotic travel.

Dreams may incorporate messages of guidance or encouragement, perhaps helping the dreamer to make decisions about future choices. They may encompass both mundane themes, such as exchanging items in a shop, and more extraordinary ones, in which the future stretches out panoramically, perhaps on the far side of a bridge or river. Certain symbols, including doors, stairways and gates, are important and universal signs of transition. They represent a threshold that the dreamer must cross if he or she is to progress and let go of the past.

Opposite: *The gateway, a universal sign of transition.*
Below: *Marriage, with its many life-changing implications, is a common dream theme.*

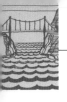
Right: Renoir's Stairway conveys powerfully the sense of passage that manifests itself as the longing to continue forging connections with our spiritual selves.

JOURNEYS

Journeys in dreams almost invariably reflect the journey through life and the ways in which we adapt to the changing scenery, or our circumstances. Usually rooted in the present, dream journeys often help to alter perspective, perhaps by illuminating life from a different angle—for example, from an aircraft.

Before travel, we assess the destination, the mode of transport and the direction or route. In dreams, these criteria represent our ambitions and how we can achieve them. Travellers are rarely in full control of their destiny: roads are sometimes blocked, and trains are delayed. Such obstacles in dream journeys usually express anxiety about failing to achieve goals, and identify difficulties that prevent us from fulfilling our potential. If a dream destination or obstruction remains important on waking, conscious consideration of recent developments or some impending change in life is necessary.

The destination symbolizes the dreamer's ultimate goal, sometimes disguised with

mythical or metaphorical associations. A westward journey (in the direction of the setting sun), for example, may represent a journey toward maturity, or old age and death, while heading east may symbolize a new youthful optimism (or resistance to ageing, if the journey is beset with diffi-

Right: A jet winging its way to foreign places may be a sign of the dreamer's hopes and aspirations—or simply of a welcome vacation in view.

culty). Sometimes, the destination is not visible, perhaps shrouded in mist or fog. It may be attainable only through a number of obstacles, both natural and man-made. The dreamer should question the origin and nature of these obstacles. Are they self-imposed? How can they be surmounted or removed? What could they represent in his or her life?

Sometimes, the destination itself may turn out to be a disappointment, or even a dead end, but the problems en route and their solutions, if any, are significant. Jung noted that journeying dreams are far more common than those featuring a destination. The mind recognizes the need for progress and uses dream journeys to help face up to decisions about the future, or acceptance of what is left behind.

The condition of the road ahead in the dream reflects the dreamer's expectations and feelings about his or her progress through life. A straight, clear road symbolizes a relatively easy path, while a narrow, rocky path clinging to the edge of a cliff represents a more tortuous route, pitted with danger and fear of failure. This symbolism is not confined to the dream world. Roads and journeys are the subject of many metaphors that reflect progress through life: one becomes "sidetracked"; it is "uphill work"; we reach "dead ends"; we "walk on a precipice"; or go "off the beaten track." The scenery through which the dreamer passes usually reflects the inner life. To dream of walking through an empty desert, for example, suggests that one's life is arid and unfulfilling, or perhaps the dreamer is lonely or infertile. The significance of dream landscapes is explored in chapter 5.

Dreams of loss of direction are bound up with fears about losing one's identity. A dream in which one searches desperately for the correct road in a strange town reflects insecurity about personal identity. The appearance of a map in this type of

Above and left: Journeys represent the dreamer's progress through life. A traffic jam like the one above implies halting progress: The dreamer is powerless and feels frustrated by his inability to advance. The clear, straight road suggests that the dreamer knows exactly what he wants and sees no obstacles barring his way.

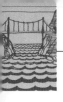

dream can represent self-knowledge. Arrival at a crossroads usually means that a decision is needed about some facet of life. Becoming trapped in a maze or circling through the same streets repeatedly are both signs that a major crisis in life is imminent, and the dreamer needs to tackle a serious problem decisively before the way ahead can become clear.

The pace of travel in dreams simply represents the speed with which goals can be achieved. If the dreamer is limping, or encumbered by a heavy load, something is holding him or her back. The significance of a dream about carrying someone is self-evident: that person (perhaps a work colleague or a relative) is perceived as a burden, and is preventing the dreamer from achieving ambitions or maintaining emotional balance. If the dreamer is running to catch up with someone, he or she is falling behind: at work, perhaps a colleague is getting ahead; in a close relationship, the friend or relative is growing apart from the dreamer. Conversely, if the dreamer is being pursued, a fear or dislike of the pursuer is indicated. Being chased by strangers or monsters suggests a fear of something in oneself, rather than a threat perceived in the outer world.

TRAINS, PLANES AND AUTOMOBILES

The mode of transport is an important factor in any journey. In dreams it represents the controlling force driving the dreamer on, so it is important to consider whether the dreamer is operating the vehicle or being driven (perhaps even "taken for a ride"). Walking, running, swimming and cycling are all proactive means of travel. These are self-sufficient modes of transport, in that we control the direction and pace. In dreams, to travel "under one's own steam" symbolizes the fact that the dreamer is in control of his or her life and of how to achieve goals.

Dream cars often symbolize aspects of the personality and of self-image. A dream about driving a fast red Ferrari suggests self-confidence, exuberance and perhaps a touch of arrogance in the dreamer. At the other end of the scale, a dream of being driven in an old rusty jalopy suggests that the dreamer has a poor self-image and does not feel in control of his or her life. If there are passengers, they may serve to influence progress, encourage the driver, or find fault.

The bodywork, steering and engine are all significant in dreams about vehicles. The bodywork represents the public image

or persona; the engine, the inner self; and the steering, the control the dreamer exerts over his or her life. A dream of driving a car with broken steering as it heads toward a dangerous cliff suggests that the dreamer feels powerless in some area of life. He or she cannot control the direction and fears a crash or disaster. A dream about mechanical failure on a deserted road miles from anywhere shows a lack of emotional confidence. The engine failure symbolizes an inner crisis: the dreamer feels unloved, and

These pages: The rider at the front of the tandem (above) has taken control of his life, choosing both pace and direction. Opposite, top, this dreamer sees life as a puzzling maze to which he is afraid to commit himself. Opposite, below, Man at Crossroads, by Mexican muralist Diego Rivera, conveys a sense of the culture shock engendered by modern science and technology. Left, "Dream cars" are often vivid expressions of personality. Background, the pointing hand and the suitcase signify a journey.

Above: *This antique locomotive balanced on a rickety track struggles to push the carriages uphill, implying the dreamer's insecurity about his or her ability to progress against great odds.* **Background:** *Steam trains in dreams symbolize male libido, Freud believed.*

the deserted road represents the fear that there is no one to turn to for help.

Cars and airplanes share some of their symbolism, mainly in areas that represent control over one's destiny. Flying in a plane still holds something of a thrill for most people, despite the widespread availability of air travel. Boarding a plane suggests a lengthy journey to somewhere far from home. In dreams, flight often represents our aspirations, or the dreamer's desire to relate to his or her higher, spiritual self—an area that may, indeed, be a long way from one's mundane, everyday concerns. For most of us, dreams of piloting a plane are exciting, even dangerous. This type of dream may symbolize a desire for rapid progress, or a wish to excel spectacularly in a particular job or enterprise. Such dreams, may, of course, simply reflect the dreamer's wish to travel!

In using public transport, we surrender any chance of controlling the vehicle, but are usually certain of reaching the desti-

nation. Trains run on rails that keep passengers on the "straight and narrow," and such dreams may hint that the dreamer's life is being run by powerful outside forces against whom he or she feels weak and inferior. This is particularly true when the train malfunctions or, as so often in life, is delayed by forces beyond the passenger's control. At the extreme is a dream of being tied to the tracks and fearing being run over. Small children want to be train engineers when they grow up (and some adults never lose their fascination with model trains), so dreams about driving a train may simply be wish-fulfillment. Freud believed that steam trains represent the male sexual urge, a theory that may gladden all those anorak-wearing, number-crunching gentlemen who indulge in the peculiarly British hobby of trainspotting.

Delays, breakdowns and missed or wrong connections are all common features of anxiety dreams, and represent fear, guilt and worry about aspects of life. A dream of running along a platform laden with luggage that slows the dreamer and prevents him from catching the train represents missed opportunities. The heavy luggage represents responsibilities, obligations or misperceptions that have prevented the dreamer from progressing, and some of these could probably be abandoned. A dream of being on the wrong train may reflect worries about the direction life is taking. The dreamer may feel that he is under pressure to do something that conflicts with an important priority. He or she may want to get off the train, but is unable to do so, signifying a lack of control in waking life. Such dreams are common when career pressures become too consuming, and the family or emotional life is suffering. Overcrowded trains that are impossible to board embody the dreamer's lack of confidence or reluctance to compete. When the train leaves, others have progressed, but the dreamer has been left behind.

Stations, airports and bus terminals are points of arrival and departure that symbolize the next phase of the dreamer's life. Busy, bustling stations can be exciting, reflecting the dreamer's confidence in the forthcoming journey. Sometimes, however, crowded stations can feel overwhelming. The dreamer may be surrounded by people rushing purposefully to catch their trains, while he or she stands still, feeling lost and unsure of where to go. This reflects a certain apprehension and anxiety about what the future holds. The dream journey may also reflect a desire to escape from loneliness. If the deserted station or airport is the point of arrival, the dreamer should consider possible causes of unease about changes in life. Perhaps the fact that no one is there to meet him at the station embodies a fear that those around him disapprove of his actions.

Journeys on boats across the sea or a river usually represent an emotional journey, as water symbolizes the unconscious mind. Boats allow us to cross water; they provide temporary security while we confront fears in the inner mind. A stormy sea symbolizes inner conflict and uncertainty. A ship's motion can also feel sensual, and may be part of a sexual dream. Sea crossings provide a number of metaphors that relate to daily life: "plain sailing," "all at sea," "shipwrecked," "high and dry."

A view of land from a boat symbolizes the contrast between the security of being on dry land and the emotional independence of being offshore; in a similar vein, a dream about going off to sea may represent a desire to leave one's family and the security of home and throw oneself on the mercy of the elements. A dream of a sea journey by night is often profound, perhaps relating to the death of the ego or a breakdown. It recalls the Greek legend about the journey to the underworld via the River Styx, where individuals must overcome their fear of death.

Above and below: Dream travel by sea takes many forms. The stolid oil tanker above plies a calm sea, making slow but steady progress. The sailboat below skims the waves at the wind's leading, but stays within sight of the shore with its reassuring lighthouse. One vessel implies stability, the other, spontaneity.

Right and below: As symbols of transition, bridges often appear in dreams, representing both connections and changes. The truncated view of Van Gogh's Bridge *(right)* suggests the dreamer's ambivalence about undertaking a new course of action whose outcome is obscure. The bird's-eye view from the Golden Gate suspension bridge *(below)* gives a clear perspective, suggesting confidence in the future and willingness to embrace change.

SYMBOLS OF TRANSITION

Bridges in dreams may represent communication and links between ourselves and others. There are many different types of bridges, and the features of the dream bridge reflect the strength of our commitment to interacting with others. Bridges also symbolize transition: we may cross a bridge to leave one phase of our life and enter a new one. The dreamer should consider what is on the far side of the bridge. A feeling of apprehension at the prospect of crossing a flimsy rope bridge, for example, reflects the dreamer's unease about embarking on a new project or relationship. The bridge—the link to the new situation—is weak, almost temporary, and this indicates a fear that, once he or she has embarked on this new phase of life, there will be no return. Facing a broken bridge symbolizes a dreamer's feelings of isolation or failure to progress in life; it reflects a sense of being stranded as one's connection and ability to communicate with others breaks

down. Alternatively, a gleaming suspension bridge with a clear view of a lovely landscape beyond reflects a dreamer's confidence in the future.

Similarly, gates and doors symbolize transitions. If a door is locked, what lies behind it? Sometimes we deliberately "lose" keys to avoid confronting something unpleasant; at other times, we are locked out, barred or excluded. Gates and doors represent opportunities, new openings, possible adventure and sometimes, secrets. Doors can open onto anything—gloomy cellars or terrifying precipices, glamorous parties or comforting, familiar rooms. Stepping through a doorway requires confidence and always provides the possibility of development or change.

Tunnels often symbolize optimism—there is always a light at the end of the tunnel, so it is usually worth enduring a dark journey through it to see what will appear at the end. Some interpreters believe that tunnels also symbolize the birth canal, and that dreams of crawling through a narrow tunnel may represent birth anxiety. Someone may experience a regression dream of being born when he or she wishes to be "reborn," to start afresh with a new outlook on life. Lewis Carroll's Alice fell down a rabbit hole and emerged into a new world that both delighted and horrified her. Her journey had been uncomfortable, but the exciting experiences at the other end made it worthwhile.

As mentioned, Freud regarded all journeys as reminders of death, and if a departure is the focus of a dream, the dream journey may well incorporate this meaning. After the death of a loved one, some people have recurring dreams about boarding a train, crossing a bridge, or heading for a gate or threshold, which reflects their desire to join the dead person. It is a common part of the grieving process, but once this urge has been confronted, the dream usually disappears.

Above: A Chinese gateway opens to a shadowed view of the walled compound beyond it. *Left: This graphic image of a railway tunnel suggests the potential for immediate access to the unconscious through the medium of dreams.* *Background: The key, symbolic of access to new areas and opportunities.*

Objects

All kinds of objects appear in dreams, from everyday household items to gift packages that hint at mystery and surprise. They may puzzle dreamers, who can think of no obvious relevance to them or their lives, yet such apparently random dream objects are usually encoded clues to significant emotions or unresolved dilemmas in the dreamer's unconscious. Many people find it easier to confront their fantasies, conflicts and relationships through symbolic language, which renders them less personal. Objectivity allows the dreamer to stand back from the problem or situation and perhaps gain a new perspective. Objects communicated by the unconscious mind may have archetypal associations, either because of their form, or simply because of their mythological, religious, or cultural affiliations.

HOUSEHOLD OBJECTS

Ordinary objects used on a daily basis in the home sometimes seem significant in dreams. Mirrors, for example, like eyes, are about observation. They emphasize the narcissistic tendencies of the dreamer, although seeing a strange face in a mirror can be a sign of an identity crisis, or even mental illness. A person walking out of a mirror suggests that new characteristics are emerging from the dreamer's unconscious. Cracked mirrors are a sign of a troubled soul, or an unwillingness to confront emotional problems.

Clocks, watches and hourglasses all suggest a preoccupation with the passage of time, or perhaps fears about aging. The ticking of a timepiece also symbolizes the beating of the human heart, and represents the dreamer's emotional life. A stopped watch suggests that the dreamer is emotionally frozen, while incessant ticking, or the hands swinging madly round the clock face, hint at a highly charged emotional state, with sentiments overwhelming the rational mind.

Although candles were once used to mark the passage of time, in dreams they relate to the intellect, or spiritual understanding. They are a source of illumination, and dreamers should note their shape and color. Candles are used in places of worship and may guide the dreamer to a source of spiritual enlightenment.

Boxes or chests, used as containers, may in dreams represent some aspect of the dreamer's life that he or she wishes to keep hidden or controlled. Boxes can also represent the womb and security, or coffins and death. Closely related in their symbolism are keys: the act of inserting a key into a locked box has obvious sexual con-

Opposite: This melancholy dreamer with all the trappings of sophistication appears to feel incongruous with his milieu, and perhaps wishes for the security of home and childhood, as symbolized by the toy duck in his glass.
Below: *A woman regards her image in a mirror, an object that may show dreamers new aspects of themselves.*

Above: The dream image of clock-faced people clutching money conjures up a number of associations, including "running out of time," "time does not stand still" and "time is money": all indicate stress and pressure. **Right:** *Treasure chests in dreams may symbolize our hopes and aspirations. They can also represent hidden, even dangerous, knowledge, like Pandora's Box, from which evil escaped into the world.* **Background:** *A television set—a symbol of communication.*

notations. As long ago as the second century BC, Artemidorus believed that "a key in a dream to him which would marry, signifieth a good and handsome wife." The English language has several metaphors for the lock-and-key concept, such as finding "the key to the problem," or gaining the "keys to the kingdom," or the "keys to someone's heart." All are related to problem solving and gaining access to an area that was once unavailable.

Dreaming of a bed suggests the unconsciousness of sleep, when one's everyday mind is put to rest and deeper levels of awareness become accessible. The bed is also a symbol of sexual intimacy, and its appearance in dreams may signify a longing or hope for union with another. Dreams of a quilt or blanket suggest the desire for warmth and protection, or the need to keep something "under cover."

Many household objects are associated with communication, including pens, pencils, envelopes, telephones and televisions. Dreams of such objects may indicate a need to share oneself with others in the form of a letter or telephone call, or to "tune in" on events in the wider world

through electronic media like television or computers. We are sociable animals, and the concept of "keeping in touch" has far-reaching implications for our mental and emotional well-being.

Dreams of household appliances like a vacuum cleaner may indicate a need to "put one's house in order," whether literally or metaphorically. The need for order and control in one's life is satisfied in part by the everyday tasks that keep our immediate surroundings orderly and attractive. Another level of meaning occurs where the dreamer is concerned about a situation or relationship that is dysfunctional or unsatisfying in some way. Here the dream of an appliance may suggest the need to restore order to one's psychic life by dealing with the troublesome condition in a concrete way.

Curtains have an obvious correlation to privacy, and dreams of them may relate to the sense of a need for secrecy, or simply a period of solitude. Alternatively, curtains or drapery may also hint at denial, that is, one's need to conceal an unpleasant or frightening reality even from oneself.

Both the needle and the spinning wheel are related to sewing and, by implication,

to clothing and other forms of protection from the elements, like bed coverings. These implements suggest the need for industry and thrift, qualities which they often symbolize in folklore. Several proverbial expressions about the needle suggest difficulty, including "finding a needle in a haystack" and "a camel passing through a needle's eye." Thus the dreamer may perceive some life situation as extremely taxing, or even impossible to resolve.

The mundane ladder is an ancient symbol of spiritual ascent, as in the Biblical Jacob's dream of a ladder reaching toward heaven. It also figures in expressions relating to material progress and achievement, such as "climbing the corporate ladder." Several essential household tasks require the use of a ladder, including repairs to the roof and to gutters that carry water away from the walls. In many senses, dreams of a ladder suggest that the dreamer has his or her work cut out.

The chimney crowns the house as a visible emblem of the family hearth and, by extension, the warmth and security of home. This is especially significant if one dreams of a smoking chimney, which signifies presence and activity. In the study of projective drawings made by children, psychologists consider the presence of a smoking chimney on a rooftop a significant sign of emotional stability.

A dream of luggage suggests travel and other kinds of ventures into the unknown. It may also be related to such expressions as "excess baggage," suggesting the need to get rid of preoccupations with the past to facilitate growth and change. Conversely, a dream of luggage may indicate a turning point in the dreamer's life—a major decision such as marriage or childbearing. A small overnight bag suggests "traveling light," while a steamer trunk implies an extended journey, whether physical or psychic, on which one will carry many personal effects and belongings.

Left: A dream image expressing modern-day concern about the projection of one's image, as symbolized by the television screen, on which shadows are often mistaken for substance.
Below: A medieval engraving of a herbalist or wise woman with distaff and spindle. It may imply that the dreamer has emerged from a wild wood into a clearing, putting a troubled phase of her life behind her, or that the thread of life is running out. The celestial orb suggests that this dream has far-reaching implications.

Below and right:
Headgear is often a symbol
of status. The feathers of
the Native American
headdress (below) mark
achievements in leadership
over a long period. The
crowns and turbans of
the kings (right, from a
medieval Book of Hours)
elevate the wearers above
the common crowd.
Opposite, below: *The fan*
is an emblem of both
femininity and perpetual
change, as symbolized by
the dancer. **Background:**
A pair of gloves, a symbol
of power.

CLOTHING AND PERSONAL EFFECTS

Since the things we wear and carry with us convey messages about our self-image, gender, occupation and place in the world, their appearance in dreams may carry a heavy weight of symbolism. This can be seen from the fact that dreams of appearing naked almost always signify feelings of helplessness, shame and displacement from our everyday feelings and activities.

Crowns and headdresses are obvious symbols of power and status. Like hats, they add authority to an individual. One may dream of being crowned as a mark of achievement, which can be a sign of where the dreamer's aspirations lie. On the other hand, a dream of having a crown or hat knocked off one's head may symbolize anxieties about status. The magnificent feathered headdress of the Native Americans of the Plains has a twofold symbolism. Like a crown, it is a sign of authority, but the feathers add another dimension in signifying wisdom. It is the chief and other notable warriors of the tribe who earn the right to wear the feathered headdress, also called the war bonnet, after years of achievement and leadership. In Western societies, feathers, especially white ones, have been associated with cowardice, as in the old expression "showing the white feather" to signify surrender. A more universal association is that of feathers with gifts, symbolizing the dreamer's desire to show warmth and love to someone in his or her life.

Rings are significant because of their circular shape, and because they represent a partnership. Rings have traditionally

stood for loyalty and commitment—admirable, if sometimes daunting, concepts—as shown by the traditional engagement and wedding rings.

The collar has several levels of significance. In ancient times, it could represent either high status and nobility or the degradation of slavery. Modern-day interpretations associate the collar with the function of the neck as a point of linkage between brain and body. Dreams of a tight collar may imply a lack of spontaneity and an anxiety about a disordered or incomplete relationship between body and mind. The necktie is associated with masculinity, and traditional Freudian analysts would interpret a woman's dream of wearing a tie as a sign of competitive envy. More contemporary interpretations would look at the word play derived from the many meanings of "tie," from tied up, as in knots of tension, to tied together, as in the union of marriage.

Gloves derive their symbolism from the hand, and their appearance in a dream may relate to one's sense of competence and power in the world—or "handiwork." In ancient times, the right-hand glove was removed ceremonially when approaching

Left: Both of these images depict people who are constrained to some extent by their formal dress. Their clothes may represent outside influences perceived as restricting the dreamer in some way.

a person of higher rank, or an altar. It is still customary to remove the right-hand glove when shaking hands, as a sign of openness and willingness for fellowship.

In most cultures, the folding fan is connected with femininity, the phases of the moon and the concept of perpetual change. Dreaming of a fan may signify the hope (or fear) of far-reaching changes in one's psychic life. A woman's dream of a fan is likely to reflect concerns about romantic love, as the fan is a time-honored means of simultaneously concealing and revealing oneself to a prospective suitor in many cultures.

Uniforms connote both status and regimentation—conformity to rigidly established codes. They are associated with policemen and military personnel, and dreams of such officials may reflect uneasiness with authority figures in one's life. Dreams of a nurse or doctor in hospital whites may suggest an interest in healing, or concern about a health problem. For some people, uniforms connote depersonalization and a loss of identity and freedom.

In a woman's dream, a purse could reflect concerns about identity; a wallet may have the same implications in a man's dream. Most people carry such essentials as identification, money, credit cards and telephone numbers in these accessories, and the loss of a purse or wallet causes real anxiety, over and above the inconvenience involved. One feels "lost" without it, especially when away from home, where he or she is unknown and may feel unsupported. A purse also symbolizes the womb.

In most symbolic traditions, dreams of jewelry and gems are related to the quest for spiritual truth. When worn in a dream by queens or noblewomen, they are attributes of the Anima. Ancient legends of jewels guarded by dragons imply the difficulties of the struggle for self-knowledge won from life experiences.

Right: Drums are ritualistic instruments, and their appearance in dreams may represent our awareness of continuity and natural rhythms in our lives. Below: Dolls, related to childhood, may simply be nostalgic symbols; they may also serve an anthropomorphic purpose in representing characteristics of the dreamer. Background: An antique piano, with associations to good times past.

TOYS AND PASTIMES

Dreams of dolls and other toys may express the dreamer's joyful inner child, or perhaps represent a longing to return to the safety and certitudes of childhood. Such objects as rocking horses, toy trains and tricycles suggest celebrations like Christmas and birthdays and may be closely tied to nostalgia for one's original home and family. In giving or collecting dolls and other toys in adulthood, the happiness of these early experiences is recreated and shared with one's children, nieces and nephews, or needy families without the means to provide such pleasures for their own children.

Dice have a place in both children's games and adult pastimes, including gaming or gambling. The die is an ancient symbol of fate, as seen in expressions like "the die is cast." Dreams of dice may relate to both good and bad fortune and to the role of chance in human experience. In modern symbolism, throwing a six in a game of dice represents victory.

Musical instruments have a wealth of meanings in dream symbolism. The flute, for example, is phallic and masculine in shape, but feminine in its high pitch and tone. The drum has a rounded feminine shape, but its deep tones are masculine, and it is associated with ritual and dancing in many cultures. Both instruments have aspects of the Animus and the Anima combined. In essence, an instrument is a form of relationship or communication and may reflect the need for self-expression of a higher order than the dreamer has been capable of in the past.

Cameras and lenses have obvious correlations to vision and point of view. Dreams of a camera may be unconscious messages about the need to sharpen one's focus on a specific goal, or, on the other hand, to take a wider view of a given situation. Cameras are also closely associated with travel and celebration. They provide lasting mementoes of milestones and happy events in the dreamer's life experience. In the hands of an artist, the camera is an incomparable tool for capturing a memorable image that can be shared with many others.

HARDWARE AND METAL OBJECTS

Machines and engines of various kinds are associated with power. In essence, they are magnified tools and suggest the ability to get things done. However, they have a negative connotation of impersonal, monotonous work, as seen in the expression "assembly line," which is the antithesis of traditional artisanship and creativity. To dream of a machine may reflect the fear of being overrun by heedless forces of destruction like the Juggernaut. On the positive side, machines have high energy and a reliable capacity for accomplishment, as seen in such expressions as "under full steam," or "in top gear." Their parts and functions may also symbolize various tasks performed by the body, including ingestion, digestion and reproduction.

Other metal objects are also associated with power and, often, with protection. Swords, for example, may be considered simply as phallic symbols, but their primary use is as weaponry. Their hilts give them a crosslike shape, and in legends and mythology—and sometimes in dreams—swords are positive forces, representing the triumph of good over evil. Short swordlike weapons including knives and daggers often suggest immediate danger, as they are used for lethal combat at close quarters. Symbolically, the short blade of the knife represents the primacy of the instinctive forces in the person wielding it, whereas the long blade of the sword implies the ascendancy of the spiritual in the swordsman.

The gun is a phallic and phobic symbol closely tied to destructive forces. Dreams of a handgun, rifle or machine gun may signify a need for authority or domination, or

link breaks, the chain is useless. If a sense of restraint predominates in a dream of chains, the dreamer should consider whether he or she feels restricted by events or individuals in his life.

The anchor is a symbol of stability and had mystic significance for the early Christians of the catacombs, who inscribed it as a sign of hope and salvation. In dreams, the anchor may suggest that one has come to a place of rest and reflection and may gain a new perspective on life.

The magnet has a mysterious power of attraction for iron and steel, and dreams of a magnet may signify that one is powerfully drawn to something or someone. The electromagnetic field also has healing properties, a fact long familiar to Eastern cultures, but only recently being discovered in the West. The concept of a benign force field may figure in the dream of a magnet, as ancient astrology related the various metals to the planets and their orderly arrangement in the heavens.

Above: *The Hero sweeps the maiden away to safety, armed with his sword, the symbol of good triumphing over evil.* **Right:** *Chains clearly imply a sense of restraint in the dreamer's life, as symbolized by this figure from an Abolitionist protest of the mid-1800s.*

the fear of such authority. A man's dream of a gun that will not fire may signify concerns about sexual impotence.

A dream of chains may connote either fear of restraint or dependency and trust. This latter aspect appears in the phrase "a chain is as strong as its weakest link." Where people depend upon one another, each must do his part: if a single

THE OUTDOORS
AND ADVENTURE

Many objects associated with the outdoors, closeness to nature and exciting—or even frightening—adventures appear in our dreams. Some of them have far-reaching archetypal significance, including the net, a symbol of those who fish in the unconscious mind, as dreamers do in sleep. It can stand both for entanglement in unresolved problems and for ensnaring symbolic "monsters" that need to be dealt with in waking life. The Chinese Tao Te Ching refers to "the net of heaven" (the network of stars and constellations), which "is wide-meshed but lets nothing through." The implication is that one must make the most of life's experiences, as each individual is a small part of a greater whole. For good or ill, we are intimately involved with the universe.

The knot is closely related to the net in its symbolism. Both are associated with the sea and with the magical concepts of binding and fettering. Fishermen in the Shetland Islands still believe that they can

*Above: The net has archetypal significance in dreams as the means whereby we attempt to "catch" or recover unconscious aspects of ourselves. It may also signify entanglement or ensnarement. **Left:** Monet's* Storm at Belle-Isle, *in which fishermen contemplate a stormy sea that prevents them from putting out, could be the dream image of a troubled psyche. The dreamer is afraid to embark on the turbulent waters of the unconscious mind.*

Right: Rockets may imply adventures into the unknown, a psychic thrust forward, or phallic energy.
Below: Wise women are common to the folklore of many cultures, whether as Witch, Crone, or Grandmother. Their meaning in dreams varies with the dreamer's life experience.

control the winds by the magic use of knots. Dreams of a knotted rope may imply either pure connection or lack of freedom through an unchanging psychic situation. In modern parlance, the phrase "tying the knot" refers to marriage, symbolizing both union and the exclusion of other choices. Life decisions of this magnitude almost always evoke manifestations of unconscious hopes and fears.

The whip is a well-known symbol of mastery, and its appearance in a dream may imply either the desire to dominate or the fear of punishment. Dreams of a whip may also suggest that the dreamer feels pushed beyond his or her limits by outside forces like an all-consuming relationship, or an overly demanding job.

Horseshoes are an ancient symbol of good luck, due to the belief that horses had magical attributes. Jung identified the horse with "the mother within us," that is, intuitive understanding of the kind that

comes to us in dreams. In some folklores, the horseshoe symbolizes good luck only when it is turned upward, as we still see on old barns and houses; if the open end faces downward, the luck was believed to run out. In European legend, witches rode broomsticks because they feared horses. Dreams of a horseshoe may also relate to a wedding: miniature horseshoes are still sometimes used in wedding cake decorations. Because its shape recalls the crescent moon, the horseshoe also serves as a fertility symbol.

The rocket is an obvious phallic symbol, but it also implies the ultimate adventure—a journey into outer space. Dreams of a rocket may imply that one is about to "launch into" a new phase of psychic growth and change, or a new realm of endeavor in the outer world. It is interesting to note that contemporary dreamers have a host of new images to provide powerful stimuli for their dreams. These include supersonic aircraft, computer terminals, video games, media icons and cellular telephones.

MYSTERY AND SURPRISE

Dreams are often about searching for someone or something vital to our happiness. A particularly powerful symbol of this sort of quest is the Holy Grail, the cup believed to have held Christ's blood. There are many legends about the search for love and truth represented by the Grail, but on a more personal level, dreamers should consider what they are searching for in spiritual and material terms. As symbols of destiny, cups may represent the dreamer's self, so the search for a cup suggests a quest for self-knowledge. If the cup is retrieved, its form is important: whether it is a jeweled goblet, a glass, or disposable plastic, it symbolizes the dreamer's self-image. Cups are classic female sexual symbols, and in a man's dream the two meanings may be entwined, as he seeks the perfect woman.

Wrapped gifts and packages suggest a pleasant surprise, and their appearance in a dream could indicate anticipation of a happy event, or the unexpected solution to a problem. On the spiritual plane, a gift may be equated with grace—an intervention by God or a higher power sacred to the dreamer to restore peace or bring guidance in a troubling situation. Since gifts express love, dreams of a gift may originate in an unconscious resolve to give or receive love, including self-love, on a deeper level than one has experienced before.

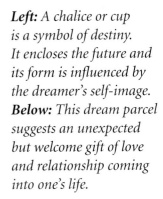

Dreams of a well may also imply mystery and surprise, as the well is a primordial image of the soul. The act of drawing water from a well is symbolic of drawing up the contents of the unconscious mind, and gazing into a well has affinities with mystic contemplation. Wells have often served as healing centers and places of worship. In Christian symbolism, they signify refreshment on the pilgrimage of life, leading ultimately to unending peace. Conversely, wells that have run dry or been boarded over may imply a loss of life energy and creative power.

Left: A chalice or cup is a symbol of destiny. It encloses the future and its form is influenced by the dreamer's self-image.
Below: This dream parcel suggests an unexpected but welcome gift of love and relationship coming into one's life.

Abstractions

Aside from the people, places and objects—familiar, foreign or fantastic—that populate all our dreams, the significance of a dream image can be strongly influenced by abstractions like colors, numbers and shapes. Shades of color set moods and can indicate emotions in the subconscious; numerical concepts can represent degrees of inner harmony or conflict; and shapes frequently allude to archetypal concepts.

COLORS

Colors are among the most basic symbols. Rooted in nature, always around us, they are inherent in our dreams. Many people claim that they dream in black and white, but dream researchers have concluded that this is unlikely. It is more probable that some dreamers suppress their memories of the colors in their dreams shortly after waking. Some researchers believe that particularly vivid colors are a sign of precognitive dreams.

Colors have individual meanings and associations for everyone—we all have a favorite color—but there are also certain universal connotations for different hues. Red, for example, is often associated with anger, passion and love, white with purity. It is useful to be aware of the meaning of the colors that appear in dreams, simply because they add an extra dimension to their interpretation. Generally, dark colors indicate a depressed or sombre mood, bright ones the dreamer's energy and vitality. Particular colors are also associated with the four faculties of the mind: white or light blue relates to the intellect; green

or brown to sensation; gold or yellow to extrovert intuition, and dark blue to introverted intuition; red or pink have to do with the emotions. When a combination of these colors appears in dreams, it is useful to be able to separate and identify them with the various functions of the mind. For example, a shuttered, dark-blue house in a dream may convey a message about a rather introverted person (the house representing the soul).

In our waking lives, colors play an important part in determining our moods, and our personal reactions to certain colors impinge, in turn, upon our dreams. Designers of both homes and clothes spend their lives trying to impress upon us the need to adapt our wardrobes and homes to changing fashions and seasons, and color is clearly vital. Red and green overwhelm us at Christmas, and navy and white, with their nautical connections, appear in the summer. Off-white or beige imply coolness during sultry summer days.

Opposite: Red usually represents passion: Here it is worn to reinforce the sensual quality of the dance.

Below: The warm colors captured in this still life by Cezánne represent a fortuitous balance of emotion and intellect. Yellow is a color of hope and an emblem of Eastern spirituality.

Opposite: The combination of green and violet at top suggests burgeoning life and transformation. Below, the vibrant gold of Van Gogh's Sunflowers evokes the sunlight for which they are named.

These associations, as well as more archetypal interpretations, all affect dreamers' visualization of colors in dreams.

Brown, the color of earth, may be associated with depression because it is a relatively dull pigment. Freud believed it hinted of an anal fixation because it is the color of excreta. A warm brown, however, can symbolize abundance (it is the color associated with harvest and cornucopias), or authenticity, honesty and simplicity (like solid wood, and the traditional monk's habit). Black, too, can be a cheerless color, signifying mourning in Western societies, and the all-enveloping blackness of a dark night that can terrify small children. Like red (for the devil and fire), black is the color of all things malevolent in Christian symbolism: it is contrasted with white (purity) and associated with the dark side of human nature. In the complete absence of light, there is no room for the light of God. Yet black also epitomizes elegance and sophistication, and can be seen as the richest of colors (as in black velvet) as well as the absence of color.

As the opposite of black, white means light, inspiration and purity. Brides wear white to symbolize their virginity, and for Christians, who visualize it as the color of Christ's robes, it represents innocence, joy and immortality. Like blue, white can color everything to infinity, in which the dreamer can become lost. In this way, it represents death: in Hindu tradition, white is the color of mourning. It is associated with self-knowledge and candor, although occasionally white can be so dazzling that we are prevented from seeing clearly.

Blue is a spiritual color, the color of the sky, which is related to the clarity and coolness of the intellect. Associated with the color of the Virgin Mary's robes in

Right: In the West, white is the traditional color of purity and innocence, as symbolized by the wedding gown and veil. The color black is associated with glamour and sophistication in women's fashions and with formal dress ("black tie") for men as well.

Christian symbolism, it thus represents chastity, eternal happiness and peace. Blue may also hint of sadness, as in the phrase "got the blues." Dark blue, the color of the sea, is linked to the emotions.

Indigo and violet hint at intuition, divination and religion. Indigo is a color of twilight and early dawn, and purple is used for religious vestments and for royal robes. Violet represents penitence in Christian tradition.

Green is the color of fertility and of new life springing from the earth. It is the most relaxing color in the spectrum and symbolizes youth and hope, love and nurture. In everyday terms, a green light means "go." Less optimistically, it is also associated with envy and jealousy ("the green-eyed monster").

Red can be regarded as the opposite of green, both visually and in symbolic interpretation. The color of raw energy, red represents vitality, passion, fire and anger. It is the color of the stereotypical vampish "scarlet" woman. Associated with the womb, red is also seen as a maternal color. Phrases like "seeing red" and "waving a red rag at a bull" show that it often represents anger. A dream of a volcano spewing glowing red lava into the sky may be about suppressed anger in the dreamer's waking life.

Gold and yellow are most obviously associated with the sun. In imperial China, none but the emperor was permitted to wear yellow, but in Christian tradition it represents humility. Yellow may relate to the intellect, self-discipline and detachment. A brilliant yellow in dreams illuminates everything, like the sun, but a paler, more sickly version is related to ill-health ("jaundiced"), fear and cowardice ("yellow-belly"). Gold is a majestic hue, the color of wealth and the glory of heaven.

Silver is associated with the moon, which symbolizes purity and feminine (sometimes mystical) spirituality.

Above: The dreaming mind often deals in numbers, which play an important role in most of the world's symbolic, mythological and religious systems. Twins may connote the number two, representing dualism, symmetry and balance. Right: The obelisk is an ancient symbol of the number one, which relates to both individuality and unity. Background: A triqueta, representing the Trinity or a harmonious family.

NUMBERS

Like colors, individual numbers have personal associations as well as archetypal meanings. Christ died at the age of thirty-three, and this number has significance for devout Christians, but it is more relevant to a thirty-two-year-old as his or her age next birthday. The early twentieth-century dream interpreter Gustav Miller believed that dreams of numbers denoted an unsettling and worrisome time in business, and Freud thought that they simply alluded to matters that could not be expressed in another way. The unconscious mind plays games with numbers, juggling them in the way that it makes puns from words to jog the dreamer's conscious mind. Numbers in dreams often refer to dates, or activities may be repeated a number of times to emphasize a point. Sometimes numbers appear in dreams in disguise. A pair of birds may alight on a windowsill, perhaps signifying the number two, or a single pillar may represent the number one. Even numbers generally represent the feminine principle, odd ones, the masculine. The shape of certain individual digits is also important in dreams: the number one, for example, is a vertical line with phallic connotations.

Many mythologies and religions place great importance on numbers. The Mayans personified ordinary numbers as representing gods, and the sixth-century Greek followers of the Pythagorean philosophy believed that numbers were divine entities. Every society or religion lays special emphasis on certain numbers; in the West, for example, thirteen is considered unlucky.

If numbers appear in your dreams, you should consider the most obvious meaning personal to you, whether it relates to a house number, for example, or to someone's birthday. If it has no immediate relevance, consider the deeper, esoteric meaning.

Zero is nothing, a void. It is universal and signifies prehistory and the all-embracing circle from which life was created. The number one is rather less nebulous. It is the first, founding principle, the source of all numbers. Vertical in shape, it has the phallic symbolism of power and the masculine principle. In dreams it often stands for oneself or isolation.

Two is about duality and balance—the two halves of an object or the partnership of a relationship. The appearance of two in a dream may be a sign of ambivalence about a particular area of life; it offers the dreamer a choice of direction, and is therefore about reflection and equality.

The number three often symbolizes a family, although in some relationships, two is company and three a crowd. It is the number of the Trinity in Christianity and Hinduism, and such figures as the Three Graces or Three Furies in Greco-Roman mythology reflect the importance of the number in ancient times. Pythagorus called three the perfect number, and it may appear in dreams as a triangle, which symbolizes fire and virility, but also, in its equilateral form, harmony and proportion.

The number four represents dependability and solidity. A symbol of Earth, it has many associations, including the four seasons, four elements and four Gospels. It is related to the square and the cross.

The number five is rare in dreams and can have very different meanings. It often represents human beings (who have four limbs and a head, as well as five senses and five digits at the end of each limb), but it can also be a magical number, related to the five-pointed star and the pentagram. The number of creativity and dynamism, it is a sign of the link between the heavens and Earth, with feet on the ground and the arms and head reaching toward the skies.

Six depicts balance and harmony. As a composite of three, it is known in the Judeo-Christian tradition as the number of creation: the world was created in six days. It was also a number sacred to the Druids and represents understanding.

Seven is sacred in many cultures. A cyclic number related to rhythm and time, it appears everywhere, from seven days in the week, to seven colors in a rainbow, the sacred seventh day, and the seven wonders of the world. It represents accomplishment in dreams, although it can also be the number of risk and opportunity, of pain and perfection.

Eight encompasses symmetry and tolerance, particularly in relation to the Buddhist eightfold path of enlightenment. If the numeral is turned on its side, it becomes the lemniscate, the symbol of infinity.

Nine is a mystic number important to Buddhists. It is the final single-digit number and signifies endings. In dreams it may symbolize pregnancy (because of nine months' gestation). Ten is the basis of the decimal system. It is also the number of law, as seen in the Biblical ten commandments. The number eleven represents intuition and self-knowledge.

Twelve, like seven, is a cyclic number related to the passage of time: twelve months in the year and signs of the zodiac. It is important in spiritual terms, too, as there were twelve disciples of Christ and twelve holders of spiritual truth. Thirteen is almost universally unlucky in Western culture, a superstition related to the fact that there were thirteen people at Christ's Last Supper, one of whom was a traitor.

Left: The five-pointed star represents humankind, the link between heavens and Earth. To paraphrase Oscar Wilde, our feet are on Earth, but our heads look toward the stars. The cosmic person depicted through the centuries signifies the axiom that All Is One.

Below: Leonardo da Vinci's Last Supper *illustrates why the number thirteen is considered unlucky in the Christian tradition: it was one of the twelve apostles present who betrayed Christ to His enemies.*

Right: The beauty and continuity of the double-helix spiral—the form of DNA—is a natural symbol of continuity and potent energy.

SHAPES AND GEOMETRY

Numbers are often related to geometric shapes in dreams. Indeed, shapes are often expressions of numbers themselves. Shapes may reflect the structure of the dreamer's inner nature. Jung noticed the recurrence of archetypal shapes like circles, squares and triangles in both the dreams and doodles of his patients. Mandalas (the Sanskrit word for "circle") are a visual metaphor for the universe and are widely used as meditational aids in Buddhism and Hinduism. As Jung's patients recovered, their dreams began to feature mandalalike circles and squares with lines radiating from a single point. Jung noticed the similarity between these and the religious diagrams used by Tibetan monks as a focus for their prayers. He regarded the mandala as symbolizing a map of the human mind, reflecting its complexity and the human quest for a complete understanding of the self. The word "mandala" has come to mean any significant shape

Below: Eggs are an almost universal symbol of fertility, and in dreams often represent the future and the potential inherent in new beginnings, including the rebirth of the Self.

that appears in the dream mind, such as a circle within a square, or geometric patterns. Often these patterns appear in the form of a garden, or the layout of a house or courtyard.

Circles represent the inner being and the self. They form enclosures that provide protection and safety from attack. Circles, which have neither beginning nor end, express perfection and represent the wheel of life moving eternally through time and space. Eggs, for example, are ancient symbols of fertility and regeneration: their shape is related to the circle. A basket of eggs in a dream, or a newly laid egg, may seem to be surreal, but may well symbolize the dreamer's hopes for a new project or phase of his or her life. The orb carried by a monarch as part of the coronation regalia is spherical: it represents not only power and wealth, but, like the egg, hope for the success of the new reign.

Spirals are ancient symbols that suggest energy and movement. Associated with labyrinths, they are about the evolution of the soul as it searches for peace and inner harmony. A clockwise spiral represents a move toward consciousness, and a counter-clockwise spiral, movement to the unconscious. Dreams about mazes often symbolize the dreamer's descent into the unconscious, perhaps against the wishes of the conscious mind, which erects defenses to prevent this exploration of the inner soul. Swastikas, ancient symbols of creative force, are related to spirals as they share a sense of movement and rotation. Spirals also appear on shells, objects related to the sea, the symbol of the unconscious.

The straight line is the antithesis of the spiral. It may represent the ego of the dreamer, or if it manifests as a long straight road, the dreamer's life. A vertical line is a symbol common to many cultures and usually indicates the male or active spirit. Objects such as sticks, rods or wands comprise a vertical line, which in its phallic sense represents fertilization. A horizontal line represents the feminine principle or a horizon dividing the conscious from the unconscious. Parallel lines, which often appear in dreams as railway lines, represent duality and separation. A dream about parallel lines may indicate that the dreamer is too conformist, confining his or her life to the route provided by the rails.

The square is the symbol of the Earth and represents solidity, balance and security. An unyielding figure, it may hint at a lack of suppleness and breadth. Such phrases as "square deal" relate to honest dependability, and are clear indicators of the shape's meaning in dreams.

Crosses, like squares, are composed of four lines, but have very different meanings. As the symbol of Christianity, the cross holds spiritual associations as the meeting place of Heaven and Earth. It also represents decisions, as compass points are indicated by a cross. Each arm points in a different direction, which may symbolize a dreamer's dilemma. An equidistant cross in a circle (such as a Celtic cross) symbolizes man in the wheel of change. In dreams a cross may simply represent a crossroads, or new point of departure.

Triangles, composed of three straight lines, are related to the threefold nature of man—the perfect balance between body, soul and spirit—and of the universe—heaven, Earth and living things. In both Hinduism and Christianity the deity takes on a triple aspect: Vishnu is creator, preserver and destroyer, the Christian God, Father, Son and Holy Ghost. Triangular shapes in dreams include huts or pyramids.

Two triangles together form the six-pointed star, with one triangle pointing upward and the other down, representing the union between the physical and spiritual sides of the dreamer: stars are symbolic of destiny. The five-pointed star is often used as a symbol of protection in magic, or it may be the symbol of man. The latter is an ancient symbol, as shown by Leonardo da Vinci's picture of a naked man spread-eagled within a star surrounded by a circle. If the star is inverted, it is said to represent evil. More generally, a dream of bright stars twinkling in the sky represents artistic or intellectual hopes.

It is important to remember that the primary meaning of any person, color, shape, landscape or object in dreams may be entirely personal. Dreams can provide answers to many of the conundrums of our lives when we learn a degree of self-awareness, explore archetypal patterns, and approach our dreams with an open mind to work with the clues that they provide.

Left: This medieval image of Christ carrying the cross incorporates a number of important symbols. The circular halo with rays reminiscent of the sun signifies holiness and wisdom. The cross as the Tree of Life is the basic Christian symbol, which may appear in dreams to guide one to a decision, or as a sign of perseverance in adversity. Below: The multitiered pagoda based on a series of steps stands for spiritual ascent to new levels of consciousness. Background: The shepherd's cross, whose four lines symbolize security.

INDEX

ACKNOWLEDGEMENTS

The publisher would like to thank Keith Hunt, for illustrations; Peter C. Gillies, for the index; and the individuals and institutions listed below, for permission to reproduce photographs on the following pages:
AKG, London: 12, 16b; **American Graphic Systems:** 100t; **Corbis-Bettmann:** 7, 10b, 13, 14t, 15t, 17t, 28t, 31br, 45t, 72t, 98t, 100b; **CorelDraw:** 8t, 30t, 52t, 53tr, 63, 67b, 94b, 95tr, 106b; **FPG International:** 8b (© James Porto 1992), 23 (© Rob Goldman 1994), 24b (© James Porto 1994), 26b (© Joyce Tenneson 1993), 27tl (© Joyce Tenneson 1992), 27c (© Rob Lang 1992), 27tr (© Dennie Cody 1993), 28bl (© Ron Chapple 1994), 28br (© Richard Gaul 1992), 33t (© Michael Simpson 1992), 34b (© Mark Gottlieb 1994), 35t (© Dick Luria 1992), 35b (© David Waldorf 1993), 37 (© Tom Wilson 1991), 38t (© Barbara Peacock 1993), 38l (© Ron Chapple 1993), 38br (© Steven W. Jones 1992), 39t (© Michael Goldman 1992), 39b (© David McGlynn 1993), 40tl (© Rob Goldman 1992), 40tr (© Steven W. Jones 1988), 42l (© Paul Ambrose 1994), 42r (© Beth Ava 1994), 44t (© Rob Goldman 1991), 44bl (© Eric Jacobsen 1992), 44br (© Joyce Tenneson 1993), 46t (© Ken Ross 1993), 46b (© Frank Chozus 1994), 47 (© Anne-Marie Weber 1994), 53b (© L.O.L. Inc. 1988), 64b (© Chip Simons 1993), 65 (© Richard Gaul 1991), 66t (© Jim Cummins 1994), 68t (© Terry Qing 1992), 69 (© Stephen Simpson 1992), 71 (© Bill Losh 1991),
73 (© Rob Goldman 1992), 74t (© Ron Thomas 1991), 74b (© Ken Ross 1992), 76bl (© Richard Gaul 1992), 76br (© G. Randall 1989), 77b (© Art Montes de Oca 1994), 78t (© Josef Beck 1992), 79t (© Ron Thomas 1991), 79b (© James Porto 1992), 81 (© Jean Paul Nacivet 1992), 82b (© Eric Schnakenberg 1992), 83t (© Peter Gridley 1992), 83b (© Charly Franklin 1994), 84t (© Michael Simpson 1994), 85b (© Dean Siracusa 1992), 87t (© Michael Hart 1989), 88b (© Gerald French 1992), 91 (© Steve Joester 1992), 92t (© James Porto 1987), 92b (© Richard Laird 1992), 93t (© James Porto 1992), 101b (© Richard Laird 1993), 104l (© David Waldorf 1993), 104r (© Ed Braverman 1992), 108b (© John Isaac 1994); © **Glass Eye Photography:** 90, 97; **London Illustrated News:** 20, 29t & l, 41; **Peter Palmquist Collection:** 106t; **Planet Art:** 11, 14l & r, 15b, 16t, 17b, 18, 21, 22, 24t, 27b, 29r, 31t &l, 32, 33b, 36, 40b, 43b, 45b, 48, 49, 51, 52b, 54t, 58b, 59t, 60c, 61t, 64t, 66b, 67t, 70, 72b, 75, 76t, 77t, 78b, 82t, 84b, 85t, 86, 87b, 88t, 89b, 94t, 95tl, 99b, 103, 105b, 107b, 109t; **Prints and Photographs Division, Library of Congress:** 19, 98b; **Saraband Image Library:** 10t, 26t, 30l, 34t, 43t, 53tl, 54b, 58t, 60l, 93b, 107t, 108t; **South Dakota State Historical Society, State Archives:** 68b; © **Jack Vartoogian:** 95b, 96t, 102; © **Charles J. Ziga:** 6, 9, 25, 50, 55, 56, 57, 59b, 61b, 62, 80, 89t, 96b, 99t, 105t, 109b. Illustrations © **1998 Keith Hunt.**